ITALIAN COOKING

Uniform with this volume

GERMAN COOKING
Nella Whitfield

FRENCH COOKING
Elizabeth Smart and Agnes Ryan

AUSTRIAN COOKING
Ann Knox

ITALIAN COOKING

Dorothy Daly

SPRING BOOKS

SPRING BOOKS
PRING HOUSE · SPRING PLACE · LONDON NW 5
Printed in Czechoslovakia

Contents

Introduction	7
Some Useful Facts and Figures	10
Flavourings, Trimmings & Spices	12
Antipasti	20
Soups	29
Pasta	49
Ravioli & Gnocchi	67
Rice	74
Polenta	90
Omelettes, Egg & Cheese Dishes	94
Fish	101
Meats	129
Poultry & Game	152
Vegetables	162
Salads	181
Sweets	184
Sauces	198
Index	221

Introduction

Before thinking about Italian cooking, it's as well to give some thoughts to the good foods native to that sunny country.

And before getting down to the food itself, give some consideration to what, in Italy, is its essential accompaniment — good wine. From north to south whether one travels by road or by rail, one doesn't travel far without seeing stretches of vineyards, and from the delightful Soave, produced in the vicinity of Verona, to the slightly spicy Orvieto of the Umbrian Hills, down to the delicate Lachrima Christi with which the visitor to Naples, Pompeii and Amalfi is regaled, there's no excuse in Italy for stinting the wine with which to cook or with which to eat the finished dish. Not all Italian wines travel well enough to allow them to be brought across to our own country, but a little patient exploration of the Italian wine shops of Soho will result in a fairly lengthy list of Italian wines that can be purchased here in England at a price sufficiently reasonable as to make it not an extravagance to use them when suggested in the recipe for a truly Italian dish, or to form the highly agreeable habit of taking a glass or two of 'Vino' with one's Pasta or Ossobuco. Make the acquaintance of your Italian wine merchant; talk to him about his various wines, ask him to suggest good wines for certain dishes; get him talking about the different wines to be met with in different parts of his beloved country — if he's a true Italian, his advice will be well worth taking, and the next time you visit his country you will order your wine by name, instead of mumbling something about 'half a bottle of that red stuff'. And in spite of the long list of 'named' varieties, your Italian wine merchant will probably point to the wisdom of buying a carafe of the local wine, for many of these local wines, though they do not travel well, are excellent when drunk in their own particular place of origin.

Not only is Italy a country of wines, it is also a country of cheeses, cheeses of a staggering variety. There is no need at all in Italy to ruin an otherwise perfect dish by the addition of two tablespoonfuls of grated 'mousetrap', nor is there any need in England nowadays to commit such a solecism when a fairly good range of Italian cheeses may be found in the best provision shops of most of our large towns. Where cheese for cooking is concerned, we may have to substitute Bel Paese, which travels well, for Mozzarella, which doesn't, and our own cream cheese for the Italian Ricotta which again doesn't care much for transportation, but where table cheeses are concerned, there's a wide variety from which to choose.

And what of the olive groves, where the silvery-grey leaves of the slender gnarled trees give an other-world appearance to the landscape? Small wonder that so many truly Italian dishes are built upon a foundation of either the fruit, green or ripened to blackness, or the oil extracted from the fruit of these trees — and remember, the use of oil in cooking does not mean that the resulting dish will be oil-y — only the badly cooked dish merits that adjective.

Wines, cheeses, olive oil, lemons, lemon juice and tomatoes (raw, cooked or rendered down into the puree or conserve we can now purchase in 'tooth-paste' tubes that allow one to use a little without wasting the balance), green, red, yellow and variegated peppers, purple egg plants, artichokes, and zucchini are but a few of the colourful basic foods of the peninsula, but they are enough to go on with.

And why, so far, no word of PASTA, that everpresent, ubiquitous Italian dish? For the reason that Pasta, whatever it may be to-day, is said not originally to have been a native of the country, but is alleged to be one of the many wonders brought home by the 13th century explorer, Marco Polo, from his travels in China. Nevertheless, although Pasta, in its many shapes and forms, may not have started off as a true native of Italy, to-day it seems as much a part of the country as an operatic tenor, and anyone wanting to present a truly Italian meal must perforce learn a few of the ways of preparing and cooking Pasta.

So much for the food and drink harvested from the land. What about the fruit of the seas that wash the shores of the long, indented coastline, all the strange and lovely fish and shellfish abounding in the waters? What of the colourful fish to be seen in the fish market in Venice, to mention but one of the famous markets? In most coastal towns of Italy fish is good and recipes for cooking it abound. English taste won't, of course, take kindly to all of them, and the mention of octopus may bring forth a horrified shudder, but few English men or women look askance at a dish of scampi or red mullet, and these are but two of a great number of delicacies piscatorial.

In the following pages an attempt has been made to offer to the English cook a selection of typical Italian dishes that can be cooked and enjoyed in her own country. It is a compilation rather than an invention, for to 'invent' four hundred 'original' Italian recipes would be not merely an impossible task but an insult to the established repertoire of Italian cooks.

Some Useful Facts and Figures

COMPARISON OF ENGLISH AND AMERICAN WEIGHTS AND MEASURES

English weights and measures have been used throughout this book. In case it is wished to translate these into their American counterparts, the following table gives a comparison:

Liquid Measure

One pint of liquid may be regarded as equal to two American measuring cups for all practical purposes.
3 teaspoonfuls equal 1 tablespoonful.
16 tablespoonfuls equal 1 cup.

Solid Measure

ENGLISH		AMERICAN
1 pound	Butter	2 cups
1 pound	Flour	4 cups
1 pound	Granulated Sugar	2 cups
1 pound	Brown (Moist) Sugar	$2\frac{2}{3}$ cups
1 pound	Rice	2 cups
1 pound	Chopped Meat (finely packed)	2 cups
1 pound	Lentils or Split Peas	2 cups
1 pound	Coffee (unground)	$2\frac{2}{3}$ cups
$\frac{1}{2}$ ounce	Flour	1 level tbsp
1 ounce	Flour	1 heaped tbsp
1 ounce	Sugar	1 level tbsp
$\frac{1}{2}$ ounce	Butter	1 tbsp smoothed off

(Tbsp = tablespoonful)

COOKING TEMPERATURES

Simmering (water)	180° F.
Boiling (water)	212° F.
Very slow oven	250° F.
Slow oven	300° F.
Moderately slow oven	325° F.
Moderate oven	350° F.
Moderately hot oven	375° F.
Hot oven	400° F.
Very hot oven	450°-500° F.

TABLE OF EQUIVALENT OVEN HEATS

(Classified according to the manufacturer)

	Slow	Moderate	Mod. Hot		Hot	Very Hot
Exact Temperature	250-325	350	375	400	425	450
Cannon (Autimo) Parkinson (Adjusto)	3-4	4-5	5	6	7	8
Flavel with Nos. Main with Nos. G. L. C. New Herald	4	5	6	7	8	9
Radiation (Regulo)	2	3	4	5	6	7
Flavel (Letter)	D-E	F	G	G-H	H-I	I-J
Main (Letter)	C	C-D	D-E	E	E-F	F-G

TABLE OF EQUIVALENT OVEN HEATS

Fahrenheit	Centigrade	Réaumur
212	100.0	80.0
200	93.3	74.6
176	80.0	64.0
167	75.0	60.0
150	65.5	52.4
122	50.0	40.0
100	37.7	30.2
86	30.0	24.0
65	18.3	14.6
32	00.0	00.0

Flavourings, Trimmings, Herbs and Spices used in Italian Cookery

Here in England the catalogue of herbs in general use is small: mint for mint sauce, or for adding to the water in which we are cooking new potatoes or peas, parsley for garnishes or for an addition to white sauce, thyme and sage as ingredients for what is collectively known as 'stuffing' for pork, veal or a bird, while spices we tend to think of as an added ingredient to Christmas cake or Christmas pudding, and not too much of them to be used for that purpose.

In the Italian kitchen, however, herbs and spices play a far more important part, and a chapter is not too much to devote to their nature and uses. Taking them alphabetically the following is a fairly comprehensive list: —

BAY: Although it is possible to purchase dried bay leaves at most herbal stores and at some chemists' shops, their flavour is nothing to be compared with that of a freshly plucked leaf, and since the shrubs grow well in tubs and, except for adequate watering need little care or attention, why not grow your own? They make an attractive addition to any garden, and even in a small yard or balcony there is room for a small tub of bay. If your house stands far enough back from the street, a tub of bay each side of the front door is attractive, and at the same time provides a useful means of adding to your flavouring ingredients.

A leaf of bay in a risotto — removed before serving — or in a casserole of meat or fish, or even as an added flavour to the Béchamel base for cream soups is an excellent idea.

BASIL: Basil is a herb little known and used in this country, and one rarely to be met with in the English garden, yet its cultivation is not difficult. It grows in profusion in Southern Italy where it is used as a fragrant and welcome addition to most dishes where tomatoes are used, chopped finely — or preferably torn into fine shreds with the fingers — and added to a green salad, and it also takes its place as a delicate and unusual flavouring in some egg dishes and soups.

In attempting to grow this delicious herb in an English garden, remember the heat and sunshine of Italy where it thrives, and choose a sunny corner of your plot or a sunny window-box for your experiment. If, in spite of all your care, it refuses to flourish, it is possible to buy the dried herb from most herb stores, but as with all dried leaf herbs, it is at best a poor substitute for the leaves of the growing plant.

BORAGE: This is a herb we in England associate mainly with wine cups, but in parts of Italy it is used as a flavouring ingredient, sometimes it finds its way into the filling for ravioli, sometimes, finely chopped, a sprinkling is added to a green salad, and its flavour combines excellently with that of cucumbers. It is a plant that grows wild on our own Sussex Downs, but if these are inaccessible to you, it is possible to purchase it at some, though not all, herb shops. It is advisable to use it quickly after it is picked, as it has a tendency to wither quickly.

BREADCRUMBS: It is an excellent idea to get into the habit of slicing thinly any left-over stale bread, drying it out in the bottom of the oven when baking, and when it is crisp grinding it into fine crumbs so that one is never without a jar of these ready at hand to be used as a coating for fried foods, or sprinkled, together with grated cheese, on top of a baked fish dish, or as a thickening ingredient for various stuffings.

CELERY: The Italian climate does not appear to produce such a deliciously crisp 'eating' celery as we are accustomed to in this country, for which reason it rarely makes an appearance in its raw state in that country, but stalks and even the inner, tender leaves are used as flavouring ingredients in soups and stews.

And here is a hint, not native to Italy, but worth remembering when celery is out of season. Instead of discarding the tougher, outer stalks, scrub these clean, wipe them dry, and cut into inch lengths. Spread on a tin and dry slowly — on the floor of a slow oven, or on top of your kitchen boiler. When quite dry, store in a screw-top jar, and use as a flavouring for soups when fresh celery is no longer available. The dried stalks can also be used as a flavouring ingredient in stews, but in this case it is best to tie them in a piece of muslin, so that they can be removed before the dish is served, as they are unattractive to the eye once they have been dried.

CHEESE: The variety of Italian 'table' cheeses is extensive, but there are three 'cooking cheeses' the names of which appear time after time in Italian recipes.

Of these three, the one best known to English cooks is Parmesan, the apparently high cost of which has alarmed more than one inexperienced housewife. Actually, in practice, this cheese works out not at all extravagantly, for its texture is so close, its flavour so concentrated that a very little of it when grated will produce sufficient to go a long way. Do not be tempted to go about the use of Parmesan the 'easy' way by purchasing it already ground. If you buy a small lump, even as little as two ounces in weight, and grate it freshly for each occasion, the flavour is richer and the cost less than if you rely on the commercially ground variety.

Another cheese frequently mentioned is Mozzarella, a cheese made from buffalo milk, which unfortunately does not stand up to export, and consequently is not to be found in this country. It is fairly safe to substitute Bel Paese wherever a recipe mentions Mozzarella, and Bel Paese is obtainable in most good provision stores nowadays.

The third cheese for which we in England need to think up a substitute is the sheep's milk cheese, Ricotta, met with in Southern Italy, a cheese that when fresh possesses a deliciously pungent flavour, but which, as with Mozzarella, does not stand up to export or long keeping. As its consistency is much the same as our own sour milk cottage cheese, although the suggestion might sound like rank heresy to an Italian cook, cottage cheese is a fairly safe substitute wherever Ricotta is prescribed.

FENNEL: The root of this vegetable, thinly sliced, forms a frequent ingredient in salads, particularly in and around Venice, where I have often mistaken it at first bite for the heart of celery by reason of its somewhat similar appearance and texture. A second bite, however, disproves this, for there is a slight flavour of aniseed to fennel, which is absent from celery.

Sliced thinly and sprinkled with salt and marinated in olive oil, fennel is sometimes served as a tit-bit at the end of a meal.

We and the French use the leaves of fennel as a flavouring ingredient far more than does the Italian cook; take for example the delicious fennel sauce served as an adjunct to boiled fish — particularly salmon, and the French use of it as a flavouring for soups and stews. But, except for the districts around Perugia and Gubbio and other cities of the province of Umbria, the stalk and leaves rarely find their way into Italian recipes. The Umbrians are fond of using fennel to flavour the stuffing used in roast sucking pig.

FISH, TINNED OR SALTED: Anchovies, sardines, and tunny are frequent ingredients in Italian cookery, and it is a good idea to keep a stock of all three in your store cupboard.

GARLIC: Yes, I know, we've all encountered that garlic-laden breath that has given rise to the legend that all Italian food is heavily laced with this odorous bulb, but legend notwithstanding, the best type of Italian cooking prescribes no more than a discreet use of this pungent member of the onion family.

It is now possible to purchase a garlic crusher, made on the principle of a potato ricer, which enables a few drops of garlic juice to be added to a dish rather than a too-coarsely chopped clove. These presses are not cheap, but in labour-saving and flavour-refinement are a worthwhile investment.

Certainly in and around Naples the use of garlic in dishes made from tomatoes and in soups is somewhat lavish, and the Neapolitans have a fondness for a dish of spaghetti flavoured with nothing more than good, fresh olive oil and garlic (here is an instance where your garlic press will give good service), but in the main, the use of garlic in Italian cooking is tempered with more restraint than rumour would have one believe.

JUNIPER BERRIES: These strike an alien note in English minds where flavourings are concerned, but used discreetly, they form an interesting addition to the stuffing for pork or game.

MARJORAM *with which may be classed the elusive herb OREGANO, mentioned in so many Italian recipes, which is the wild marjoram similar to that which grows on our English Downs:*

Either the sweet marjoram, which is easily procurable from a herb shop, and which many of us grow in our gardens, or the wild is a welcome addition to many Italian dishes, to soups, and fish dishes, while a pinch in an Omelet aux fines herbes does not come amiss. As with all herbs, the fresh product, when obtainable, is infinitely preferable to the dried.

MINT: In English cookery it usually means the mint sauce we eat with roast lamb, or a sprig or two to be boiled with new potatoes or with spring peas, and that, except for the Mint and Currant Pasty of Lancashire is the extent to which we use it. The Italian cook makes a far wider use of the herb, particularly in and around Rome where it makes a fairly frequent appearance as a flavouring to soups, fish dishes, stews and salads.

MUSHROOMS: Dried mushrooms — uninteresting though they may look hanging in strings in an Italian provision shop — are excellent used in small quantities in many soups and sauces. Before use they should first be soaked in warm water to soften them, and added to the dish 15 to 20 minutes before serving time. Overcooked they tend to lose their flavour and their texture is flabby.

MYRTLE: The sweet-smelling myrtle of Southern Italy and Sicily has a stronger odour than our English variety. It is used less in Italy as a flavouring ingredient than on the island of Sardinia.

OLIVE OIL: Frequently, all-too-frequently, alas, one meets the one-voyage-abroad traveller who complains of Italian food that it is 'much too oily' and one feels that the cooking of the country has once again been let down by the wrong kind of restaurant, for though the Italian cook uses olive oil lavishly for deep frying, for salads, as a dressing for pasta, etc., provided the oil and the cook are of first quality, the resulting dish is not oily in the objectionable sense, but rich, fragrant and delicious.

The oil, however, must be olive oil of the best quality, and the temptation to substitute an anonymous product making its appearance under the name of 'frying oil' is one to be sternly resisted. Until you know your oils, it is advisable to spend your money on a named brand, the San Remo, for example. Get accustomed to using a good oil, to recognising its flavour and its cooking qualities, and later you may safely experiment with less well-known brands, but even then, insist that the oil you use must be olive oil, for just as the grey green foliage of the olive tree is an essential feature of the Italian landscape, so is the oil of its fruit an essential feature of Italian cookery.

PARSLEY: It is used lavishly by Italian cooks, in soups, in salads, as an ingredient for the stuffings for meats, vegetables and the various forms of ravioli. If you are able to obtain a package of seeds of the true Italian parsley, try growing this instead of or in addition to our English variety. The leaf is flatter, thinner and less curly, so that for decorative purposes our English plant may be preferable, but the flavour of the

Italian parsley is considerably stronger and more poignant and for that reason I would recommend its use whenever possible.

PINE NUTS: Do experiment with these, which are stocked by most vegetarian stores. A few chopped and added to a sour-sweet sauce, or used in place of almonds in cake-making, or instead of salted almonds to be served with drinks, will reward your courage.

ROSEMARY: It is a herb we in England tend to think of in conjunction with the word 'Remembrance' or even, alas, as an ingredient for hair tonic; as a cooking ingredient it seems alien to our taste. However, chopped and used sparingly, since it is extremely pungent, either fresh or dried it is delicious sprinkled over sauté potatoes during cooking, or again used cautiously to flavour a roast of veal, pork or lamb. In some of the Italian food markets you will see rolled fillets of meat already prepared for roasting and lavishly trimmed with this herb, but for English taste a little of it goes a fairly long way.

This again is a herb that can be grown in one's own garden, and once again you'll find that a pinch of the fresh is worth a peck of the dried.

SAFFRON: Is used mainly to produce a delicate yellow colour in some rice dishes, rather as in Cornwall it is used to produce a similar yellow tint in the saffron buns for which that county is noted.

The dried stamens of the Autumn Crocus give us the true saffron and when one remembers that there are but three stamens to one flower, it can be realised what an extensive cultivation of the flower is necessary to produce a very little supply of saffron. If you are working with the dried stamens, take three or four of these, bruise them to a powder, and allow them to steep in a little hot water or soup for five or six minutes before adding the strained liquid to the dish you are colouring. A quicker method is to purchase, literally, a thimbleful of powdered saffron from one of the many Italian grocery stores to be found in Soho, and experiment by adding it a pinch at a time until you have obtained the desired colour.

The flavour of saffron is so delicate that it is apt to be obscured by the stronger predominating flavours of the dish so that, preferable though it always is to use the true product, in this case, the substitution of a manufactured imitation does not materially affect the taste of the finished dish.

SAGE: Although this herb is used less in Italian cooking than in our own, it is occasionally mentioned in a recipe. Because of its heavy under-taste, it is to many lovers of Italian cooking less attractive than basil or wild marjoram.

SALT: Here is a case where I would urge you to forsake the nicely packed, beautifully ground commercial salt and to try the experiment of using the sea salt that can be purchased from the provisions department of most big stores. There are wooden salt mills that can be used at table for adding this salt to cooked food, and once tried, these are usually preferred to the trickle — or in our damp climate, the frequent lack-of-trickle — of commercial salt from a salt shaker or salt spoon.

SPICES — a few of the most common.

Cinnamon: Instead of confining its use to cakes and apple dishes, try the occasional pinch in a meat or vegetable dish.

Cloves: Some Italian cookery books prescribe a pinch, a very modest pinch of this aromatic herb in stewed meat or meat sauces, and it is a tip worth trying.

Coriander seeds: Keep a small jar of these in your spice cupboard and try one or two crushed as a flavouring for roast meat.

Fennel seeds: These are used for flavouring far more than are the leaves and stalks of the raw plant and there is a specially delicious kind of salami, native to the city of Florence which takes its name 'finocchiona' from the fact that fennel seeds are predominant in its flavouring ingredients.

In some parts of Italy and Sicily these seeds are used also as a flavouring for dried figs.

Nutmeg: By all means continue to use this spice as a flavouring in milk dishes, but do experiment now and again with the wider use of it — a pinch in a meat stew, or in potato soup, or in any dish using spinach makes a welcome addition.

Pepper: If you have not yet forsaken the commercially packaged ready ground pepper for the pleasure of grinding peppercorns in your own pepper mill, I cannot too strongly urge you to do so without delay. The improvement in flavour is almost unbelievable.

TARRAGON: Is a herb we use little here in England, and for that reason it is not always easy to procure it in this country, but a leaf or two in a salad is a reward for the effort of running it to earth, while the delicate flavour of tarragon vinegar once acquired is preferred by many to the cruder taste of plain malt vinegar in salads.

THYME: Although in Southern Italy and in Sicily one often comes across this herb growing wild, and after a sprinkling of rain finds the air drenched with its fragrance, it is not used as much in cooking as it is in England. It can, however, be used in restricted doses wherever oregano has been suggested if this is unobtainable or difficult to find.

TOMATOES: Where tomatoes are concerned, as a general rule the tinned varieties imported from Italy are preferable to our own fresh, local grown tomatoes.

In any dish calling for raw tomatoes, ours are excellent, but for cooked dishes, sauces, stews, soups, etc., I would every time recommend the tinned, peeled tomatoes. The tomatoes grown in Italy are larger and softer than those we grow here, their flavour is richer, and their colour deeper. One of the most popular and easily-obtainable brands is the CIRIO, but there are several others to be purchased in provision stores if this particular brand is not available.

Concentrated tomato paste is another ingredient appearing again in Italian recipes, and after years of experimenting, a method of packaging this has been evolved that is practical and non-wasteful, for it can now be purchased in metal tubes, rather after the fashion of tooth-paste, so that when a little has been used, the tube can be sealed and the remainder kept without danger of spoiling. Previously this paste used to appear in microscopic tins which had a fiendish knack of defeating even the best tin-opener, particularly if the cook happened to be working against time. Another former method of packaging was in small blocks wrapped in oiled paper, which, because of the high degree of concentration of the paste, necessitated a fair amount of pounding to reduce them to a usable consistency. It is still possible to purchase the paste in these forms, but the tubed variety is infinitely easier to handle.

Do not fall into the trap of using this paste too lavishly, for while a little is excellent, too much can result in an overflavouring that tends to kill the other flavours of any dish.

Antipasti

Antipasti is the name given to the large variety of tit-bits, or hors d'oeuvres which, in a truly Italian household, are served as a prelude to pasta or soup. They may consist of a few wafer-thin slices of salami with a garnish of a couple of anchovies and a few black olives, or they may be considerably more elaborate, but whatever their nature they must be interesting to look at and appetising to taste. Some of the following suggestions may fill you with apprehension; for instance, boiled rice combined with grated carrots, or the slice of ham to be eaten with an ice cold slice of honeydew melon, or with a couple of ripe figs, but taste and try, and you'll probably come back for more.

ANTIPASTI MADE WITH RICE

Really delicious antipasti can be concocted starting with a basis of plain boiled rice.

Allow one tablespoonful of rice per person, and boil in salted water as directed under the heading of 'RICE'. Drain, and before it is quite cold season with a tablespoon of olive oil to each tablespoonful of uncooked rice, freshly ground black pepper, more salt if needed, and a teaspoonful of lemon juice or wine vinegar, plus a suspicion of finely chopped or crushed garlic, or a few shavings — very thin — of onion. Allow to become quite cold, then mix with any of the following, or a combination of two or three of them:

Grated raw carrot — using half as much carrot as rice.

Finely shredded raw green peppers — quantity as for carrot.

Tunny fish broken small with a fork, equal quantities of fish and rice, and even better with the addition of one anchovy per tablespoonful of tunny fish.

Finely chopped green olives, half as much as rice.

Whole black olives, four or five per tablespoonful of rice.

Minced cold chicken, equal quantities with rice.

Mushrooms, raw or cooked in equal quantities.

Fresh peeled shrimps or prawns, or if available, scampi, and to enhance these, add also a generous amount of freshly chopped parsley and a few cooked green peas or French beans.

Chopped celery hearts, finely chopped fennel, finely sliced preserved artichoke hearts in equal quantities with the rice, are three other alternatives, and with these try the addition of a few blanched and chopped almonds or pine nuts.

Using the foregoing suggestions as a basis, you should be able to utilise left-over boiled rice to good advantage to produce an interesting hors d'œuvre.

HARICOT OR BUTTER BEANS WITH FISH

It is now possible to buy cooked butter beans in tins, or alternatively you may use the small white haricot beans, remembering however that these need soaking overnight, and then boiling for quite three hours the following day before they are tender. Whichever you decide to use, drain and marinate with a little under a tablespoonful of olive oil to a tablespoonful of beans, seasoning with salt, pepper and a little grated onion, and a little lemon juice or vinegar. Serve with equal quantities of flaked tunny fish, very cold.

FENNEL ANTIPASTO

head of fennel
3 tablespoons olive oil
1 tablespoon lemon juice
freshly ground black pepper
salt

Wash a head of fennel, and soak in very cold water for two or three hours to allow it to become crisp. Slice thinly, and pile on a dish. With it hand the above dressing, into which the fennel is dipped before eating. Mix well together and serve cold.

STUFFED FENNEL OR CELERY

Wash the tender stalks of either of these, soak in cold water to allow them to become crisp, and before serving spread with cottage cheese, pounded anchovies, or a combination of the two.

OTHER WAYS WITH FENNEL

Try combining thinly sliced fennel with thinly sliced crisp red radishes, or with thinly sliced unpeeled cucumber, in each case serving with a dressing of oil, lemon juice, pepper and salt, and a sprinkling of parsley, or mint finely chopped.

FORTUNATA RUOCCO'S COLD PEPPER ANTIPASTO

To each person allow:

1 pepper (assorted colours make the finished dish more attractive)
1 small teaspoonful best olive oil
½ lemon
a scraping of garlic

Prepare your peppers by baking them whole in a fireproof dish placed in a larger dish with water halfway the height of the dish containing the peppers. Cook until the skins are wrinkled — about ¾ hour Regulo 6.

Cool slightly, peel off the thin outer skin, cut in two and remove all the seeds. Slice thinly, and arrange on a serving dish, alternating the colours if you have been able to procure peppers of varied colours. Sprinkle with a scraping of garlic, and marinate with olive oil. Cool thoroughly before serving, and allow half a lemon per person when the finished dish is served.

Hot Antipasti

In addition to the galaxy of ideas for cold antipasti, or hors d'œuvres, our Italian friends are fond of serving delicious little hot tit-bits that take the same place in the repast as the cold antipasti, and are a trifle less chilling on a cool day. Here are suggestions for some of these, which can also make their bow as rich little savouries to be served with drinks.

CHICKEN TARTLETS

Into a little rich Béchamel sauce, say a breakfastcupful, mix two tablespoons grated Parmesan, and quarter of a pound or more of cold cooked chicken, cut into small pieces, a few chopped mushrooms, and a slice of lean ham cut small. Mix well together, and use as a filling for tartlets.

CHICKEN LIVER TARTLETS

This time, impregnate your cupful of Béchamel with chopped chicken livers that have been cooked in a little Marsala, and to this add chopped mushrooms and seasonings. Mix well and use to fill small pastry tartlets.

STUFFED MUSHROOMS

Choose the small 'button' mushrooms, and allow three or four per person.
Peel, and remove the stalks, setting the stalks aside to be added to soup stock or tomato sauce — DON'T waste them, whatever you do, they are far too good a flavouring. Sauté the mushrooms in hot butter; meanwhile heat the contents of a small tin of anchovies, and when the mushrooms are cooked, place a curled anchovy inside each mushroom (the dark side is the side to receive the anchovy). Serve on toothpicks while still very hot.

ANCHOVY TOAST
TO SERVE 4

Mash to a paste the contents of a small tin of anchovies, mixing with a little melted butter. Prepare some slices of bread about 4 inches by 2 inches, and toast on one side only. On the other side spread the anchovy paste fairly thickly, sprinkle with grated Parmesan, and if liked a few chopped green olives. Brown under a hot grill and serve while piping hot.

HOT ANTIPASTO MADE WITH GREEN PEPPERS

For each person allow:

1 green pepper
1 peeled tomato
half a dozen capers
two or more anchovies

a suspicion of garlic
a few drops of oil
from the anchovies

Remove the seeds from the peppers after having sliced off the top; stuff the cavity with one peeled tomato to each pepper, add a suspicion of garlic, two or more anchovies, half a dozen capers, and a few drops of the oil from the anchovies. Replace the top of each pepper.

Place in a fire-proof deep dish, place in a medium-hot oven (Regulo 6), bake 45 minutes, basting at intervals with the balance of the oil from the tin of anchovies and a little hot water.

Serve before or in place of soup, very hot.

These are even more attractive if baked in individual fire-proof dishes.

PANDORATO ALLA ROMANA
Fried bread in the Roman fashion

For this recipe, allow one or two half-inch slices of bread per person, and remove the crusts so that your slices are about 3-inches square.

You will need also a little warmed milk, one or two beaten eggs, depending on the number of slices, salt for seasoning, and oil for frying.

An hour before starting to cook the slices, spread them in a single layer in a large flat dish and sprinkle them with warm milk, and then with sufficient beaten egg to soak the bread without making it soggy. Leave for an hour, then lift each slice gently with a spatula and fry in hot oil, first on one side then on the other until golden brown.

FRIED BREAD WITH ANCHOVIES

Allow one or one and a half slices of bread per person; cut the slices about half an inch in thickness, remove the crusts and cut in two, lengthways. To each strip of bread allow a little BEL PAESE and half an anchovy and for the whole dish allow one or two eggs depending on the quantity of bread to be prepared. You will need also pepper and salt for seasoning, flour and oil for frying.

On half the number of strips of bread spread a layer of BEL PAESE, and on that lay half an anchovy cut into small pieces. Season with pepper, and cover with the second slice.

Heat the oil in a pan, and meanwhile dip the sandwiches first of all in water or a little milk, then in flour and finally in beaten egg, and fry quickly, first on one side and then on the other until golden brown. Serve very hot.

PANDORATO ALLA CREMA DI FORMAGGIO
Fried bread with cheese cream
TO SERVE 4

6 slices of bread, half an inch in thickness, with crusts removed and cut in two lengthways

$\frac{1}{4}$ lb. Gruyère cheese
$\frac{1}{4}$ pint milk, or a little more

a walnut of butter
2 eggs, separated

Whip the whites of eggs. Having prepared the strips of bread, dip them first in water or a little milk, then in flour, then in the whipped egg whites; fry them in hot olive oil and when golden brown, lay in a flat fireproof dish and cover with the following cheese cream:

CHEESE CREAM FOR PANDORATO ALLA CREMA DI FORMAGGIO

Cut the cheese in small pieces and place in a basin, and cover with the milk and leave for quite an hour, by the end of which time the cheese will have softened. Place it in a double boiler, add the beaten egg yolks and stir with a wooden spoon until the whole is mixed well and has become a thick cream. Remove from the fire and stir in a knob of butter the size of a walnut.

Spread this cream over the slices of fried bread and serve hot, garnished with sprigs of parsley.

CROSTINI ALLA NAPOLITANA

For each person allow two slices of bread, half an inch thick, with crusts removed and cut in two lengthways, and for each slice of bread allow one anchovy, a little BEL PAESE and half a tomato skinned and with the seeds removed. Allow a little oregano and pepper for seasoning.

Fry the pieces of bread in hot oil on one side only, then arrange in a single layer in a greased flat fireproof dish, fried side uppermost. On each slice spread a layer of BEL PAESE, half an anchovy cut small and a thin slice or two of tomato, and finally sprinkle with oregano and black pepper and a few drops of olive oil.

Cook in a hot oven for ten minutes to allow the cheese to melt. Serve very hot.

FRIED GREEN OLIVES

3—4 large Spanish olives per person
a thick slice of bread with the crust removed
1 anchovy to each 4 olives
flour
pepper and salt
batter and oil for frying

Peel the olives in a spiral so that you can remove the stone without breaking the flesh; soak the bread in a little water, and when it has become saturated, squeeze it dry in the hand; one slice should be sufficient for half a dozen anchovies. Remove the bones from the anchovies and pound them in a mortar, together with the bread, a few drops of olive oil and season them with freshly ground black pepper. When they are reduced to a paste, stuff the cavities of the olives with the mixture, then dip in flour, and after that into a thin batter, and fry in hot olive oil. Drain well before serving.

Soups

Soup forms an integral part of the daily diet of Italy, and the variety of Italian soups is considerable.

Starting with a basis of chicken or meat stock, we have several plain, clear broths, of the consommé type, we have the ever-popular 'minestrone' type, where the stock is laced with an assortment of vegetables, eked out with dried peas or beans, and occasionally meat, and there are the various forms of 'pasta in brodo'.

The Italian verb 'minestrare' — to serve up soup — derives from a similar Latin verb 'minestrare' which has the fuller meaning of 'putting food on the table', and it must be admitted that when a bowl of really good minestrone is placed before one, it has the appearance of a meal in itself, and could well serve as such, since there seems to be no end to the many ingredients that can find their way into this tasty and typically Italian dish, and all to its betterment.

'Pasta in brodo' is the term applied to a generous portion of any of the large variety of pastas, cooked and served in hot broth, and taking the same place in the menu as the 'pasta asciutta', or dry pasta, cooked and served with various sauces, with which we have dealt in the section headed 'PASTA'.

The variety of fish soups in the Italian cook's repertoire is far greater than in our own, and although cream soups and purées were originally more used in France than in Italy, with the passage of years a fairly large number of recipes for these have found their way into Italian cookery books, adapted and amended so that they now pass as very nearly native to the country of their adoption.

Where the consommés, the minestre, and the pasta in brodo are concerned, although the family stockpot is not absolutely essential, it is strongly to be recommended if time and space permit. There are, it is true, some truly excellent chicken and beef bouillon cubes now obtainable in good provision stores, but the best of these is but a substitute for the broth resulting from the operation of a well-run stock-pot. For that reason I am starting the recipes of this section with 2 suggestions for Soup Stock.

STOCK FOR CLEAR SOUP

- 2 pounds lean beef - shin of beef is excellent
- 2 quarts cold water
- 1 small onion
- a few stalks of celery
- 4 cloves stuck into the onion
- 6 whole peppercorns
- 1 bay leaf
- salt, pepper, and a sprig of parsley

Cut meat small, place in a stew pan and cover with cold water and bring slowly to the boil. Skim off any scum that rises to the top with a perforated spoon. Cover stewpan closely and let it simmer slowly for 6 hours or rather more. Strain, cool and remove fat. Replace in pan, adding onion stuck with cloves and celery cut small, parsley, peppercorns and bayleaf. Simmer for a further 20 minutes after bringing to the boil. Add salt and pepper to taste. Strain through a cloth.

This is an excellent basis for any clear soup, to which may be added 'pasta' for a dish of 'pasta in brodo', rice, or pearl barley.

HOUSEHOLD STOCK POT

- 3 quarts of cold water
- 3 pounds of meat; trimmings from steak, bones, etc. and the addition of a ham bone or bacon knuckle bone is excellent
- 1 small onion stuck with 4 cloves
- 6 peppercorns
- parsley
- 1 stalk celery, chopped small
- salt and pepper

This is a stock that may be used as a foundation for many kinds of soups or sauces, for casserole dishes, etc.

Place meat in a stewpan and cover with cold water and bring slowly to the boil, skimming well. Cover and simmer for 5 hours, or longer, add balance of ingredients and simmer one hour more. Add salt and pepper to taste, being chary of adding too much salt if you have among your meat a ham or bacon bone. Strain and set aside to cool. Remove the fat before using.

Brought to the boil once daily, this stock will last for several days without spoiling.

CHICKEN BROTH
TO SERVE 6

1 boiling fowl	1 pinch thyme
2 carrots	a dash of nutmeg,
1 onion	salt and pepper to taste
3 stalks celery	
1 tablespoon chopped parsley	4 quarts of water

Place all ingredients in saucepan, bring to boil and skim; lower heat and simmer for 2 hours or until fowl is tender. Remove fowl, strain soup through a fine sieve, allow to cool and remove fat. Reheat. This is a good basic soup for any of the varieties of pasta in brodo.

Try it with Cappelletti filled with the following mixture:

the breast of the boiled chicken chopped fine	1 egg plus one egg yolk
$\frac{1}{2}$ lb. cottage cheese	3 tablespoons grated Parmesan
2 tablespoons butter	
salt and pepper	

Mix well together and use as filling for Cappelletti. Drop into boiling chicken broth five or six minutes before serving.

Where cream soups are concerned the starting point is a good, rich Béchamel sauce, thinner than used when intended purely as a sauce, but made with care and using the best ingredients, butter, flour, milk and seasonings. The following is a good, reliable recipe for a Béchamel to be used as a basis for cream soup to serve four people:

$1\frac{1}{2}$ to 2 ounces butter	$1\frac{1}{2}$ pints hot milk
2 tablespoons flour	pepper and salt

Melt the butter in a small saucepan or in the top of your double boiler, but do not allow it to brown. Add the flour and blend well together, stirring constantly to prevent its going lumpy. Add the hot milk slowly, continuing to stir. When thickened, allow to cook very slowly for a further 15 minutes, otherwise the taste of the flour will predominate. Add a little extra milk if it looks like becoming too thick, and if you are unfortunate enough to have it go lumpy, do not hesitate to pass it through a strainer, though if the flour and butter are well blended and the mixture is stirred constantly lumps should be conspicuous by their absence.

Once your Béchamel is properly blended and while it is 'maturing' in the top of your double boiler, you have time to prepare the vegetables for the particular cream soup you have in mind.

A time and washing-up saver is to make the Béchamel from start to finish in the top of your double boiler, rather than using a separate saucepan for the preliminary cooking and then transferring it to the top of the double boiler once the blending is completed.

One small and permissible economy that is often an improvement in flavour is to eke out the quantity of milk by substituting for one-third or one-quarter of it the hot water from a saucepan of cooking vegetables. Potato water is excellent; so is the water in which Brussels sprouts or celery are being cooked, but here it is as well to test the liquid for saltiness before adding it to the Béchamel, rejecting it if it is too highly salted, unless you are prepared to eat an over-salted soup.

A REALLY GOOD MINESTRONE
TO SERVE 6

1 pound of salt pork cut small
2 quarts water, or better, beef stock
2 tablespoons finely chopped parsley
1 clove crushed garlic if liked
1 tablespoon butter
1 small cabbage
2 carrots, diced
½ lb. haricot beans, soaked overnight
½ lb. peas — before shelling — shelled
a few French beans
4 tablespoons rice
grated Parmesan
pepper and salt

Place cut up pork in water or stock and bring to the boil before adding parsley, garlic and chopped vegetables, peas and beans. Allow to boil gently for 2½ hours, then add rice and cook for a further quarter of an hour. Season to taste. Serve with a layer of Parmesan cheese sprinkled over the soup in the tureen.

MINESTRONE No. 2
TO SERVE 4

¼ lb. salt pork cut in small pieces
1 large or two small onions
2 quarts water
1 large carrot
1 head celery
½ a small spring cabbage
½ a lettuce
½ pound tomatoes
a handful of French beans, cut in pieces
1 cupful shelled green peas
1 small tin sweet corn
salt and pepper to taste
½ cupful of small macaroni - elbow macaroni, pastina (rice-shaped macaroni) or alphabet macaroni, small stars, or any of the small types

Fry the pork in a little lard until it is slightly brown; add onion cut small and cook till golden brown; add water and bring to the boil; add carrots and celery cut into small pieces; add shredded cabbage and lettuce, beans, peas and corn, salt and pepper to taste. Cover and allow to cook gently for about 1½ hours. Twenty minutes before serving add the macaroni. Serve hot and with the soup hand-grated Parmesan to be added at will.

MINESTRONE No. 3
TO SERVE 4

1½ quarts of water
1 lb. French beans, or two cups shelled peas
4 potatoes — medium size
½ lb. tomatoes, peeled and cut into small pieces
salt and pepper to taste
2 cloves garlic crushed
2 tablespoons chopped fresh basil, or if this is unobtainable 2 tablespoons chopped parsley
1 teaspoonful tomato paste
grated Parmesan
¼ lb. vermicelli

Heat water to boiling point and add beans cut in pieces, or peas, together with the potatoes cut small and the tomatoes and seasoning. Cook together until vegetables are tender — about 25 minutes — then add the vermicelli and cook for a further 15 minutes or until the pasta is 'al dente'. Mix together the crushed garlic, basil or parsley and tomato paste with a spoonful or two of the soup to make a smooth paste, and mix with the balance of the soup, stirring well to ensure that it is well blended.

Serve with plenty of grated Parmesan.

LENTIL SOUP WITH DRIED YELLOW LENTILS
TO SERVE 4

½ lb. dried yellow lentils — soaked overnight
1 quart stock
I ham or gammon bone

2 medium sized onions chopped finely
2 tablespoons olive oil
2 stalks of celery cut fine

Drain lentils and add to stock, and gammon bone, bring to the boil, simmer gently in a covered saucepan for 1½ hours. Remove bone and pass soup through a food mill or sieve.

Heat oil in a heavy pan and in it cook the celery and onion gently for ten minutes.

Add to the soup and serve very hot.

VEGETABLE SOUP WITH MEAT BALLS

TO SERVE 6

2 quarts stock
2 stalks of celery
2 or 3 carrots
2 medium sized onions
1 turnip
1 tablespoon chopped parsley
1 medium size tin tomatoes
salt and pepper to taste

Bring stock to the boil and add vegetables and cover. Cook gently together for 2 hours, then strain through a sieve, bring to the boil and add:

1 medium sized carrot cut in wafer thin slices
1 large or two medium sized potatoes diced
1 cupful fresh or frozen peas
2 tablespoons rice
1½ dozen Polpetti *(see below)*

Allow to boil, not too quickly, for twenty minutes, and serve hot, handing grated Parmesan cheese to be added at will.

POLPETTI

Meat Balls

TO SERVE 4

1 pound lean beef passed through mincer
2 eggs
2 tablespoons grated Parmesan — optional
chopped parsley
3 slices of stale bread soaked in milk to cover it for 10 minutes, and then squeezed dry in the hands
salt and pepper
1 clove garlic, crushed

Having soaked and squeezed the bread so that all liquid is out of it, mix with the meat, lightly beaten eggs and seasonings. Having floured your hands, take a little of the mixture between them, and roll into a ball about the size of half an egg. Flatten them slightly, and fry on both sides in hot olive oil; allow to drain for a few minutes before adding to the soup.

BROWN LENTIL SOUP
TO SERVE 4

- ½ lb. brown lentils
- 1 onion finely chopped
- 1 clove garlic crushed
- 1 heaped tablespoon finely chopped parsley
- 4 tablespoons olive oil
- 1 medium size tin tomatoes
- salt and pepper to taste

The lentils for this soup are the khaki-coloured whole lentils, NOT the orange-coloured dried lentils which require longer soaking.

Cook the lentils in 2 quarts of boiling, slightly salted water for an hour; strain — but don't throw away the liquor — and set on one side. Replace liquor in saucepan, bring to the boil and add parsley, onion and garlic, and when boiling furiously add the oil and allow to boil fairly briskly for a further ten minutes. Add strained tomatoes; replace lentils and boil gently for twenty minutes more. Serve very hot.

SPINACH SOUP
TO SERVE 4

- 1 lb. spinach - before cooking
- 2 tablespoons olive oil
- 1 clove garlic, crushed
- 2 tablespoons flour
- 2 pints water, or better, chicken stock

Wash, cook and purée spinach.

Heat oil in heavy pan, add crushed garlic and when brown remove. Blend in the flour, add puréed spinach and water; bring to boil and cook gently for half an hour. Serve with croûtons of toast and grated Parmesan.

MINESTRA CRÉCY
TO SERVE 4

4 medium sized carrots (cooked in boiling salted water and passed through a food mill)	1½ pints beef stock 4 tablespoonfuls rice Salt and pepper to taste 1 teaspoon sugar

Bring stock to the boil, add rice and boil for 20 minutes; just before serving, add puréed carrot, sugar and a knob of butter.

SPINACH SOUP
TO SERVE 4

½ lb. spinach, weighed before cooking 1 tablespoon flour	2 tablespoons butter 1½ pints meat stock or milk

Wash spinach in several waters, cook gently in the water adhering to its leaves after the final washing plus a small pinch of salt. Cook rather longer than usual, and reduce water until spinach is nearly dry, then pass through a sieve or food mill.

Meanwhile heat butter in pan, blend flour and slowly add milk or stock and bring to boil, slowly add spinach purée, mix well and serve hot with snippets of toast.

A SLIGHTLY RICHER SPINACH SOUP

Proceed as directed in previous recipe, but at the end of 30 minutes cooking add the following mixture:

    2 yolks of eggs, lightly beaten
    2 tablespoons grated Parmesan
    salt and pepper to taste

Blend together and stir into boiling soup, allowing eggs to curdle slightly and serve immediately.

ZUPPA PAVESE
TO SERVE 4

For this really nourishing 'meal in itself' soup, you need a quart of clear chicken broth, into which at the end of its cooking time one egg at a time is thrown into the boiling soup for each consumer, stirred rapidly while it 'poaches', and removed to its individual soup bowl while the other eggs are similarly treated.

ALTERNATIVE METHOD FOR ZUPPA PAVESE

If you do not mind your eggs very lightly poached, place a half-inch slice of toasted French bread in each individual soup bowl, and on to it break an egg very carefully so as not to break the yolk. Over this pour the boiling soup, and serve immediately.

ZUPPA PARADISO
TO SERVE 6

This recipe, given in Rose L. Sorce's *La Cucina*, is just too good not to be included.

- 2 quarts good soup stock
- 4 tablespoons breadcrumbs
- nutmeg
- 4 eggs separated
- 4 tablespoons grated Parmesan
- pepper and salt

Bring soup to a boil, slowly add the following mixture a spoonful at a time, boil 5 to 8 minutes and serve.

Beat the egg whites till stiff, add beaten yolks and beat till well blended, add cheese, breadcrumbs.

STRACCIATELLA
One more soup with eggs
TO SERVE 4

- 2 eggs
- 1 tablespoon grated Parmesan
- 2 teaspoons fine semolina
- 1½ pints chicken broth

Beat eggs, and blend with semolina and cheese, add a cupful of cold broth, and beat well. Bring the remainder of the broth to the boil, and slowly add the egg mixture, beating with a fork or whisk; allow to cook slowly for four or five minutes before serving. The eggs will appear as little flakes or 'rags' in the soup.

CHESTNUT SOUP
TO SERVE 4

- ½ lb. chestnuts
- 2 pints stock, or mixed stock and water
- 1 bay leaf
- 1 slice lean ham
- 2 cloves

Score the chestnuts across the pointed end, and bake in a moderate oven 10 to 15 minutes, after which it should be simple to remove the outer and inner skins.

Peel and put to cook slowly with the water and ham and seasonings, for 40 minutes or slightly longer. Pass through a sieve or food mill and serve with snippets of fried bread.

VEGETABLE SOUP
TO SERVE 4

- 3 large onions
- 1 lb. ripe fresh tomatoes
- 1 clove garlic crushed
- 2 tablespoons olive oil
- 2 outer stalks celery
- 1 large carrot — cooked
- a few green peas or French beans
- 1 quart hot water

Heat oil in heavy pan, chop vegetables and cook in oil till slightly brown; add hot water gradually and cook together for half an hour. Pass through a food mill or sieve before serving.

ZUPPA ALLA FOUBONNE
TO SERVE 4

- 2 large leeks
- 2 carrots
- 1 slice ham
- 1 quart meat stock
- 2 large onions
- 1 yellow turnip
- 1 ounce butter

Heat butter in heavy pan, and in it place chopped vegetables and ham and cook gently until lightly browned. Add stock and cook together 40 minutes. Pass through a sieve or food mill, replace on heat and boil for a further 5 minutes. Serve with snippets of toast and grated Parmesan.

LETTUCE SOUP
TO SERVE 4

- 2 heads of lettuce — preferably cos lettuce
- 1 tablespoonful olive oil
- 1½ pints salted water
- 1 clove garlic, crushed
- grated Parmesan
- croûtons of bread

Wash lettuce, shred finely and boil until tender in boiling salted water. Heat oil in heavy pan, allow crushed garlic to cook for three minutes, remove garlic and add oil to swiftly boiling lettuce a few minutes before serving. Serve with snippets of bread, black pepper and with it hand a bowl of grated Parmesan.

MARROW SOUP ALLA NAPOLITANA
TO SERVE 4

- 1 medium sized vegetable marrow or 1 lb. zucchini (the tiny marrows about 4-inches or 5-inches in length)
- 1 tablespoonful lard
- salt and pepper to taste
- water
- 4 eggs
- 4 tablespoons grated Parmesan
- 2 tablespoons chopped parsley
- 1 teaspoon chopped fresh basil if obtainable
- 2 slices toasted bread

Cut the marrow into slices, and having heated the lard in a stewpan, add marrow, pepper and salt, and when it has cooked a few minutes but before it has started to brown, add sufficient water to cover. Cover the pan and cook gently until the marrow is tender (about 20 minutes).

Beat the eggs, add the Parmesan, parsley and basil, and add to the marrow mixture. Mix well, keep hot for a few minutes, but do not allow to boil or the eggs will curdle.

Serve in warmed soup bowls with croûtons of toast.

GARLIC SOUP
TO SERVE 4

4 cloves garlic, crushed
1 quart clear stock
2 tablespoons chopped parsley
2 tablespoons olive oil
4 tablespoons grated Parmesan
croûtons of toast

Heat oil in stewpan and in it sauté garlic for two or three minutes, add stock and simmer for half an hour. Strain into soup tureen, adding parsley and cheese at moment of serving, with croûtons of toast.

CHEESE AND ONION SOUP
TO SERVE 4

3 large onions
1 teaspoon flour
salt and pepper
2 ozs. butter
1 quart hot stock

Use a heavy pan for this soup. Heat butter until it begins to brown, add onions thinly sliced, and sprinkled with flour, fry briskly, turning with a wooden spoon to make sure all are cooked until they are brown rather than gold coloured. Add heated stock little by little, stirring all the time, add salt to taste, and a generous helping of freshly ground black pepper, and allow to boil for twenty minutes with saucepan uncovered.

Pour into heavy earthenware tureen, covering the surface with a raft of half-inch slices of stale bread or toast, over which sprinkle a thick layer of grated Parmesan, or a mixture of Parmesan and grated Gruyère cheese. Place in very hot oven so that cheese melts and turn golden. Serve immediately.

CHEESE AND ONION SOUP
Alternative method of serving

While your soup is cooking, toast three or four slices of French bread, and place in layers in a soup tureen, with a mixture of grated Parmesan and grated Gruyère cheese between each layer, and for added richness, a little butter.

When the soup has finished cooking, pass through a sieve, and pour over the layers of bread and cheese, and let it stand in a medium oven for ten minutes before serving.

HARICOT BEAN SOUP
TO SERVE 4

- ½ lb. haricot beans — soaked in water overnight
- 1 clove garlic, crushed
- 3 pints water
- 1 tablespoon olive oil
- pepper and salt to taste
- 4 heaped tablespoons chopped parsley

Cover the beans with water, bring to the boil and cook slowly for at least three hours.

Towards the end of the cooking time, heat the olive oil, and to it add the crushed garlic and parsley and cook together for five minutes.

Pass beans and the water in which they have cooked through a sieve or food mill, return to the saucepan, and stir in the garlic mixture. Serve hot with snippets of toast, and if liked, hand with the soup a dish of grated Parmesan.

CREAM OF TOMATO SOUP
TO SERVE 4

3 ozs. butter	1 tablespoonful chopped parsley
1 tablespoon flour	1½ pints beef stock
6 large tomatoes or 1 medium sized tin of tomatoes	½ wineglass full of cream
1 large or 2 small onions	grated Parmesan croûtons of bread toasted

Heat the butter in a heavy pan, and in it cook finely chopped onions until yellow, and flour and blend together, then add tomatoes, skinned and seeded if raw, strained if they are the tinned variety, and the chopped parsley. Season with salt and pepper and allow to cook over a slow heat, stirring all the time; after three or four minutes add stock, bring to boil and allow to cook gently for half an hour. Pass through sieve or food mill, re-heat, adding a little more stock if it seems too thick. Into a soup tureen place the cream and a knob of butter. Pour over this a little of the purée and beat with an egg whisk before adding the remainder. Serve garnished with croûtons and grated Parmesan.

CREAM OF MUSHROOM SOUP
TO SERVE 4

Prepare a Béchamel Sauce as directed under 'SAUCES' but using 1½ pints of hot milk, instead of just 1 pint, so as to avoid a too-thick consistency. Meanwhile, prepare the following:

¾ lb. mushrooms, chopped finely	1 wineglassful of sherry
1 tablespoonful chopped parsley	1 clove garlic pepper
2 ozs. butter	salt
½ pint chicken stock	nutmeg, if liked

Heat the butter, and in it allow the crushed garlic to cook for a few minutes; remove, and add the mushrooms, cut small, and allow to sauté gently until cooked; add the wine and bring to a bubbling boil; reduce the heat, add the parsley and seasonings and cook gently for a few minutes before adding the stock. Bring to the boil before amalgamating with the Béchamel, which should be keeping hot in the top of your double boiler. Serve very hot.

FISH SOUPS

We in England are not given to preparing fish soups, but in Southern France and in Italy these are immensely popular, and for that reason, a few recipes ought rightly to appear in any compendium of Italian cooking.

Where your Italian cook says casually 'take a selection of fish', it has to be remembered that in his selection can be included a great many fish that are not native to our waters, nor easily obtainable in this country, such as octopus, lampreys (a variety of eel), calamari or squid, scampi. But we in England can still, given a little ingenuity, produce 'a selection of fish' that should produce a fish soup that is tasty and nourishing. Try combining sole with prawns or shrimps, a few scallops, a little smoked haddock, or smoked cod fillet — just let your imagination work and let your eye wander around the fishmonger's slab.

ZUPPA ALLA MARINARA
Sailors' soup
TO SERVE 4

About two pounds of assorted fish, and DON'T leave the heads or skins at the fishmonger's, but bring them home and cook them with a bay leaf and a few peppercorns and a sprig of parsley in about two pints of water, until the fish is cooked; strain, and here is your 'stock'.

- 1 small onion cut in small pieces
- 1 stalk of celery cut small
- 4 tomatoes, peeled and cut in pieces
- 1 oz. butter
- ½ a wineglassful of white wine
- 1½ to 2 pints of stock prepared as suggested

Heat the butter in a stewpan and in it cook the onion until it is golden yellow, then add the celery, tomatoes, pepper and salt and allow to cook together for a few minutes before adding your assortment of prepared fish, any shell fish shelled, and other fish boned and cut in pieces; add the stock, cook together for twenty minutes and serve with snippets of toast or fried bread.

ZUPPA DI PESCE ALLA GENOVESE
Genoese fish soup
TO SERVE 4

- 2 lbs. of assorted flat and shell fish, prepared and, in the case of the flat fish, cut in pieces; saving the heads, skins and bones to make stock by cooking with two pints of water, a bay leaf and a few peppercorns
- 2 tablespoons oil
- 1 or 2 stalks celery
- 1 bay leaf
- ½ wineglassful dry white wine
- 2 anchovies
- 1 clove of garlic
- 1 medium sized onion
- 1 tablespoon chopped parsley
- 1 pint cleaned mussels

Heat the oil and in it brown the chopped onion, add the chopped celery and parsley, and the anchovies cut small, the crushed clove of garlic and the wine and cook together two or three minutes; add the prepared fish, with the exception of the mussels and the stock, and cook together for twenty minutes; about twelve minutes before serving, add the cleaned mussels and continue to cook until all are opened, then serve the soup immediately, with slices of crisp toast or freshly fried bread.

ZUPPA DI PESCE DEI PESCATORI DI POZZUOLI
Fish soup made by the Fishermen of Pozzuoli

From Pozzuoli, once one of the chief commercial ports of the Mediterranean in the days of Roman domination, and previously one of the most important Greek cities of the region, and now not much more than a fishing village, the fishing fleet goes out each year for a fishing season in the waters of Santa Marinella. The villagers help the fishermen with their nets, and it is the custom for the fishermen to prepare, at sea, a delicious fish soup, which they share with the villagers. This is a soup you won't be able to make at home, one you won't be able to taste, unless you happen one day to be lucky enough to join this fishing fleet during their summer migration from Pozzuoli to Santa Marinella. But imagine the scene, the rough old-fashioned stove on board the boat, the earthenware pot in which, with plenty of water, an assortment of freshly caught and cleaned fish is cooked, with a few tomatoes, a clove or two or garlic, a few spoonfuls of oil, and a coarsely chopped red pepper; cooked together for twenty minutes or so, then served in earthenware soup plates, with lumps of home-baked bread brought by the villagers to the fishing fleet.

ZUPPA DI PESCE ALLA SIRACUSANA
Fish soup as prepared in Syracuse
TO SERVE 4

Another fishing town, Syracuse, where carp swim lazily in the spring into which Arethusa is said to have changed when pursued by the river-god Alpheus, and where, later on, Nelson put in for a sufficiently long time to write one of his famous letters to Emma Hamilton before proceeding to his victory at the Nile. A famous fish soup in served in this pleasant Sicilian town.

2 lbs. assorted fish, the heads, skins and bones of which are to be used to make 2 pints of stock	1 stalk celery
	2 tablespoons oil
	salt, pepper
	1 tablespoon chopped parsley
	1 bay leaf
1 medium sized onion	4 or 6 tomatoes
1 clove crushed garlic	1 wineglassful white wine

This is a fish cooked in the oven. In a fireproof casserole large enough to hold the entire mixture, place your prepared fish, the larger pieces cut small, together with the chopped onion, parsley, laurel leaf, celery cut small, tomatoes skinned and cut up, crushed garlic, oil, wine and sufficient of the prepared fish stock to cover well. Season with salt and pepper, put the lid of the casserole on and weight it down if necessary to ensure a tight fit, and place in a moderate oven for 40 minutes. Before serving, remove the bay leaf. Serve with toasted or fried bread.

Pasta

The Italian term *Pasta* covers a multitude of various shapes and forms of what we in England tend to lump together in our minds under the heading of *Macaroni* or *Spaghetti*.

For centuries now *Pasta* has formed an integral part of the Italian diet, but whether or not it originated in that country is open to question. One theory is that it was among the many curiosities and wonders brought back by the traveller Marco Polo when he returned to Italy during the 13th Century after years of travel in the Orient, and in an account of his travels there is a description of the Chinese making a kind of dough which they cut in strips and dried in the sun, which strips he refers to by the Italian name of *Lasagne*, the name used to this day in Italy for one of the broad, flat ribbon-type *Pastas*.

Earlier than Marco Polo, however, there is a reference to *Pasta* in Italian literature, in the Life of the Blessed Hermit William, a holy man who lived around the year 1200, which rather discounts the Marco Polo legend.

It looks as though we are safe to assume that *Macaroni* has as good a chance of being native to Italy as *Noodles* have of being of Chinese origin; the name given to the kind of *Pasta* matters less for the purpose of this book than the various ways of cooking the product.

A word first of all about the various types of *Pasta* to be met with in Italy. Starting with the fine string-like vermicelli, too fine to have a bore through its centre, the tubular types come in all widths from the regular and familiar *Macaroni* and *Spaghetti*, to the three-inch lengths of *Canneloni*, three-quarters of an inch in diameter which, after a preliminary cooking in boiling water are stuffed and re-cooked in various ways, and served up with sauce, or with cheese and butter.

There are the fancy shapes of *Pasta*, Shells, Elbows, Cartwheels, Twists, even Alphabet Letters, and there are the various flat types, the narrow *Noodles*, the broader *Tagliarellini*, progressing to the broad *Lasagne*, and there are also the tiny rice-type grains known as *Pastina*, and small star-shapes used as a garnish for soups. The variety is infinite and the possibilities of cooking the various types into tempting dishes are endless.

Cooking Procedures

Provided one remembers a few simple rules, nothing could be much simpler than the cooking of *Pasta*.

1. See to it that you use a large utensil, a really capacious saucepan in which is an ample quantity of really boiling water — allow at least a gallon of boiling water per pound of pasta, and to each gallon add a tablespoonful of cooking salt. Before attempting to add the *Pasta*, see that the water is at a proper boil, and add the *Pasta* slowly so as not to let the water go off the boil, for once the temperature of the water drops below boiling point you are running the risk of having your *Pasta* turn into a soft, rubbery mass, instead of the desired separate strands or pieces, depending on which variety of *Pasta* you are cooking.

   If you are using the long, uncut *Spaghetti* or *Macaroni*, don't spoil the Italian appearance of your finished dish by breaking the *Pasta* into shorter lengths; don't get alarmed if at first the long ends stick out of your saucepan of water, once the submerged part has been heated through it will soften sufficiently for you to be able to persuade the long ends to follow suit.

   One reason for the emphasis on using a large enough saucepan is the need to allow for the 'frothing' that takes place when once the *Pasta* itself reaches boiling point; lower your heat a trifle when this occurs, but not sufficiently to let the water drop below boiling point. From time to time run a fork or spoon around your saucepan to loosen any stray ends of *Pasta* that may adhere to the bottom or sides of the utensil.

2. Whatever you do, don't fall into the error of over-cooking your *Pasta*, and where cooking time is concerned, you may have to go through a period of trial and error before you discover the correct cooking time for your own particular taste.

   The true Italian likes to be able to bite his cooked *Pasta:* he will tell you it must be 'al dente' (to suit the tooth), but while it must certainly not be soft enough to dissolve in the mouth, it must need only the tenderest of 'bites', such as you might give to — shall we say — a piece of Shrove Tuesday pancake. The cooking time will vary with the different varieties and thicknesses of *Pasta*, and it is a fairly safe maxim in the early days of *Pasta*-cooking to study the instructions given on the package of whichever type you choose, and to cook your *Pasta* a minute or so less than the time suggested, then fish out a small piece and test it for yourself either by biting through it, or by pressing it between two fingers. A few experimental 'trial runs' will soon give you a guide to your own best cooking times. The following table will be helpful in a broad sense, but your own experience will eventually stand you in better stead than any instructions.

3.   TABLE OF COOKING TIMES
(Approximate only)

Ordinary spaghetti . . . . 8—12 minutes
Very thin spaghetti, vermicelli . . . . . . 6—10 minutes
Long macaroni . . . . .10—12 minutes
Macaroni shells, wagon wheels etc. . . . . 8—12 minutes
Broad noodles such as lasagne . . . . . . 6—9 minutes
Medium noodles — tagliatelle . . . . . . 4—6 minutes
Alphabet macaroni, pastina (the ricelike
   macaroni used in soup), small stars, etc. 5—7 minutes
Rigatoni or gavatoni (very large macaroni) 10—12 minutes

And remember, the home-made *Pasta* needs usually no more than half the length of time to cook in comparison with the bought varieties.

4. To make sure that the cooked *Pasta* will have no slimy outer covering, it is an excellent idea to 'blanch' it as soon as it is cooked by removing it from the heat, and before draining it through a colander, adding a cupful of cold water to the boiling mass. Stir rapidly after the addition of cold water, then drain immediately through a colander, and, once drained, piled on a warm dish.

5. Having transferred your *Pasta* to a warmed dish or bowl, add whatever Sauce you have prepared and serve immediately, handing at the same time a bowl of grated Parmesan cheese, to be added to the taste of the consumer.

How Much Pasta Per Person?

It is difficult to suggest quantities of *Pasta* per person, for while one pound of pasta might be ample for half a dozen people, there are addicts to whom a personal share of half a pound might not be too much, while others might abstain from tackling more than two ounces. A fairly 'safe' allowance is three ounces per person, plus an added three or four ounces for every sixth person, to allow for that little more an addict might demand.

The following recipes will give you an idea of some of the many ways you can serve this typically Italian food once you have mastered the simple art of preparing your *Pasta* by its initial cooking in boiling water.

These all come under the category of *Pasta asciutta* (Dry *Pasta*) to distinguish them from *Pasta in Brodo*, or Pasta served as an addition and an essential ingredient of certain broths and soups.

A RECIPE FOR HOME-MADE PASTA

Although there are excellent commercial brands of pasta in the various shapes and sizes, if you are a good pastry maker and have time to experiment, you may care to try your hand at making pasta for yourself. If you do, remember that the cooking time for the home-made variety is considerably less than that required for the packaged types — 5 to 7 minutes is all that is necessary.

You will need a fairly large pastry board, and a longer-than-usual rolling pin.

The following quantities will give you sufficient tagliatelle, the most usual type of home-made pasta, for six people.

> 1 lb. flour
> 2 or preferably 3 eggs
> a pinch of salt
> lukewarm water

Pile your flour in a mound on your pastry board, making a well in the middle into which break your eggs, adding salt, and to start with a couple of tablespoons of lukewarm water. Fold the flour over the eggs and water and knead until the liquid is used up. If the paste is too stiff, add a little more water, but be careful not to 'drown' it. When the paste can be formed into a fairly solid ball, its consistency is right. You should now knead it, flouring your hands lightly from time to time, and flouring the board, for at least ten minutes; then, dividing it into two portions start the rolling process. It will need quite ten rollings and the board and roller should be lightly floured between rollings. Finally it should be thin enough, metaphorically speaking, to read the newspaper through it. Spread a floured cloth over the back of a chair and lay the paste over it while you proceed similarly with the other half. When both sheets are rolled thin, leave them to dry out for half an hour, after which roll them up as you would a Swiss roll, or pinwheel biscuit mixture, and with a sharp knife cut across the roll at intervals of a quarter of an inch or less. Lay them on a floured cloth until you are ready to cook your tagliatelle, and remember, 5 to 7 minutes in boiling salted water will be ample.

A useful hint — if you have difficulty in finding a really long roller for pasta, a length of broomstick makes an excellent one, and for drying the pasta, again a length of broomstick resting on two chairbacks, so that the pasta can hang over a cloth draped over the broomstick, is a useful dodge to remember.

TAGLIATELLE ALLA CREMA
TO SERVE 6

1 lb. tagliatelle cooked in the approved fashion	3 eggs
	4 ounces butter
	pinch of nutmeg
8 tablespoons grated Parmesan	pinch of salt
	1 pint milk
2 tablespoons flour	

Place four tablespoons of the grated cheese with the flour in a saucepan and mix slowly with the milk and a pinch of salt and nutmeg. Place on a slow heat and stir with a wooden spoon until it thickens, add a nut of butter and blend well, then remove from the fire, add the remainder of the butter and the balance of the grated cheese, and finally, when it has cooled a trifle, the beaten yolks of the three eggs. Whip the egg whites separately and fold into the first mixture. Add the cooked and drained tagliatelle to the sauce, place in a greased earthenware or oven-glass dish, and allow to cook in a medium oven for quarter of an hour.

SOUFFLÉ OF TAGLIATELLE
TO SERVE 4

1 lb. tagliatelle	6 tablespoons Parmesan — grated
1½ teaspoons flour	
3 ozs. butter	
¾ pint milk	salt
	a pinch of nutmeg

The home-made pasta made with eggs is preferable for this, though the commercially made spaghetti may be used. Cook in boiling salted water in the approved manner, remembering that whereas the bought variety will need 10 to 12 minutes, the home-made will need no more than five.

Meanwhile prepare the following sauce:

Melt butter in a saucepan, and before it begins to turn brown, blend in the flour and add milk slowly. Stir until it thickens and allow to cook over boiling water for a further 12 to 15 minutes, season with salt, pepper, nutmeg and the grated Parmesan, mix well and remove from the heat. Separate eggs, beat yolks lightly and add to the sauce when it has cooled a little, otherwise the yolks may curdle. Whip egg whites stiff and fold into the sauce. Have ready the cooked and drained tagliatelle, combine with the sauce, slowly, so as to ensure it is really well mixed. Place in a buttered soufflé dish and cook in moderate oven for 20 minutes. Serve in the dish in which it is cooked.

TAGLIATELLE WITH ANCHOVY AND TUNNY FISH
TO SERVE 4

- ¾ lb. tagliatelle cooked in the approved manner
- a 6-oz. tin of tunny fish
- 3 or 4 anchovies
- 2 tablespoons olive oil
- 1 clove garlic
- 1 tablespoon freshly chopped parsley
- ½ pint good stock

Heat oil in a heavy pan, add garlic and cook for two or three minutes, add tunny and anchovies broken into small pieces or pounded, add parsley and cook for four or five minutes. Season with salt and pepper. Add stock slowly and bring to boiling point.

Pour over cooked tagliatelle and mix well.

SPAGHETTI CON SALSA DI VONGOLE
Spaghetti with Clam Sauce
TO SERVE 6

1 pound spaghetti cooked in the approved manner. When cooked and drained pour over it hot Clam Sauce (See recipe under 'SAUCES') and serve with or without grated Parmesan cheese.

FETTUCINE WITH MEAT SAUCE AND CHEESE
TO SERVE 4

Fettucine are our old friends, home made tagliatelle, hiding, so to speak, under a pseudonym, the name give them in the district around Rome. For this dish you need the following ingredients:

- 1 lb. fettucine
- 4 tablespoons grated Parmesan
- ½ pint or rather more brown sauce (see 'SAUCES')

When the fettucine are cooked and drained, place in a heated deep fireproof dish, and cover with the meat sauce and the grated Parmesan, lifting the fettucine with two forks to ensure that it is completely masked by the sauce. Serve with a bowl containing more grated Parmesan, to be added at will.

SPAGHETTI WITH MEAT BALLS
TO SERVE 6

- 1 lb. spaghetti or macaroni, cooked as directed
- 1 small onion
- 1 or 2 cloves of garlic, crushed
- 3 tablespoons olive oil
- 1 large tin tomatoes
- 1 tablespoon tomato paste
- ½ pint water
- 1 tablespoon brown sugar
- a good pinch of oregano if available, or failing this a pinch of dried thyme
- pepper and salt to taste

Meat Balls:

- 1 lb. lean beef passed through the mincer
- 2 thick slices white bread
- 1 small onion
- 1 tablespoon chopped parsley
- 3 ozs. grated Parmesan
- 1 egg
- salt and pepper to taste

Soak the bread in water, squeeze dry and mash with a fork, and to it add the onion chopped finely, the parsley, ground beef, cheese and seasonings. Beat the egg lightly and combine with the foregoing mixture; shape into small balls — this amount should make about 12 — and fry in hot fat. Drain and set aside.

Heat the oil in a heavy pan, add chopped onion and crushed garlic and cook till golden; add strained tomatoes, tomato paste thinned down with a little water, the balance of the half pint of water, sugar, oregano, pepper and salt; lower heat, cover and cook slowly for an hour.

At the end of an hour, add the meat balls, cover pan once more and allow to cook slowly for another half an hour before serving over the freshly cooked spaghetti.

With this dish hand a bowl of freshly grated Parmesan, to be added at will.

ELBOW MACARONI PIE
TO SERVE 6

- ¾ lb. elbow macaroni cooked in the approved fashion
- ¾ pint tomato sauce (see recipes for 'SAUCES')
- 4 tablespoons grated Parmesan cheese
- ½ lb. cooked meat, chopped finely
- 2 eggs
- short crust pastry sufficient to line and top your casserole

Grease an earthenware or oven-glass casserole and line with pastry. Mix together your cooked macaroni, tomato sauce, cheese and chopped meat and lay on top of pastry. Beat eggs lightly and pour over the mixture. Cover with short crust pastry, and bake in moderate oven for half an hour, or until crust is brown.

Serve hot.

This with a simple salad makes a fairly sustaining meal.

BAKED MACARONI WITH CHEESE
TO SERVE 4

1 pint milk
salt and pepper to taste

½ lb. elbow macaroni
½ lb. Cheddar cheese

Partly cook macaroni in boiling salted water — drain. Scald milk, stir in macaroni, add pepper and salt, grate and add cheese. When well blended, transfer to fireproof casserole and bake 30 minutes in moderate oven, stirring gently after about 10 minutes to make sure it is not sticking to bottom of casserole.

SPAGHETTI WITH BUTTER AND CHEESE

One of the simplest and at the same time one of the most delicous macaroni dishes this, and one for which any of the various forms of pasta may be employed.

For each person allow:

3 to 4 ozs. pasta
1 tablespoon or more of grated Parmesan cheese

1 really generous lump of good butter

The method of cooking pasta has already been described in detail.

When cooked, blanched and drained, stir the butter and cheese into the dish of pasta, allow to melt and serve immediately, handing at the same time a dish of the grated cheese so that more may be added at will.

BAKED MACARONI WITH SOUR CREAM
TO SERVE 4

8 ozs. elbow macaroni
¾ lb. finely chopped cooked ham
½ pint sour cream
4 eggs
salt and pepper to taste

Cook and drain macaroni. Separate eggs. Beat yolks and to them add cream, salt and chopped ham. Add drained macaroni. Pile into buttered casserole. Whip egg whites stiffly and fold into mixture. Bake 30 minutes in moderate oven. *Regulo 5.*

SPAGHETTI WITH HAM

For each person allow:
tagliatelle, or any form of pasta particularly liked
½ oz. butter
3 to 4 ozs. spaghetti
2 ozs. of ham, or better, if you can purchase it in your vicinity, the raw ham that is so popular in Italy

While your pasta is cooking in boiling salted water, cut your ham into long, thin strips and sauté in the butter in a heavy pan. When the pasta is blanched and drained, combine with the ham and serve immediately.

SPAGHETTI WITH OIL AND GARLIC
TO SERVE 2

½ lb. spaghetti
4 tablespoons best olive oil
at least 2 cloves garlic, crushed
a generous pinch of basil
salt to taste

While your spaghetti is cooking, heat the oil in a heavy pan, add crushed garlic and basil, and cook for two or three minutes so as to allow the oil to become thoroughly impregnated with the flavour of the garlic.

When the spaghetti has been cooked and drained, pile in a heated dish, add the oil and garlic mixture, blend well, and serve with freshly ground black pepper and generous helpings of freshly ground Parmesan.

SPAGHETTI WITH GREEN OLIVE OIL SAUCE
TO SERVE 2

½ lb. spaghetti, cooked in approved fashion, then piled in a heated dish, and served blended with the adjoining sauce
4 cloves garlic, chopped finely or crushed
4 tablespoons olive oil
at least 4 heaped tablespoons finely chopped parsley

Heat oil in a heavy pan; add garlic and allow to brown slightly, add chopped parsley and simmer gently for five minutes. Pour over cooked and drained spaghetti, mix well and serve with grated Parmesan and black pepper.

Three Typically Sicilian Recipes

SPAGHETTI WITH ANCHOVIES
TO SERVE 4

1 lb. spaghetti or 'shells'	1 small tin anchovies (about a dozen fillets)
just under quarter of a pint of good olive oil	8 tablespoons grated Parmesan cheese
1 clove garlic	salt and pepper

Heat your oil in a heavy frying pan, and when hot add garlic, crushed, and fry until it is brown, then remove. Chop anchovies into short lengths, add to hot oil and cook for a couple of minutes, stirring with a wooden spoon. Add plenty of black pepper, but add salt with caution, remembering the saltiness of anchovies. Add this to a dish of cooked and drained spaghetti, topping with the grated Parmesan cheese, and serve immediately.

SPAGHETTI WITH FRESH FENNEL SAUCE
TO SERVE 4 OR 5

1 lb. spaghetti	1 lb. fennel
4 tablespoons olive oil	1 large or 2 small onions
1 cup cold water	1 lb. fresh sardines, pilchards or sprats
6 ozs. dried breadcrumbs	
1 tablespoon pine nuts or blanched almonds	1 tablespoon sultanas or seedless raisins

Clean and bone fish.
    Clean fennel and cook for 15 minutes in about a quart of boiling water. Drain and chop small.
    Heat olive oil in a stewpan and cook in it the chopped

onion until it is a golden colour, add fish, cook gently for 10 minutes, stirring frequently; add fennel, sultanas and nuts, cold water and seasoning and allow to simmer gently for 10 minutes.

Place breadcrumbs on a fireproof plate below a hot grill for a few seconds to brown.

Meanwhile cook the spaghetti in the approved method. When cooked and drained, place in deep, warmed dish, pour over half the fish and fennel sauce and half the breadcrumbs and mix well. Then pile on balance of fennel mixture and top with remainder of breadcrumbs and serve very hot.

MACARONI WITH BROCCOLI
TO SERVE 4

1 lb. elbow macaroni
$\frac{1}{4}$ pint olive oil

1 lb. young broccoli

While the macaroni is cooking, clean the broccoli, break into small pieces, and cook 10 minutes in boiling salted water. Heat oil, in a heavy frying pan, drain and add broccoli, and fry lightly for 3 or 4 minutes.

Grease a casserole, sprinkle with grated Parmesan. Pile into this the cooked and drained macaroni, and over it pour the broccoli and oil. Mix well. Sprinkle with more grated Parmesan, and place in a hot oven for 5 minutes. Serve very hot.

SPAGHETTI WITH BACON, EGG, AND ONION
TO SERVE 4

3 to 4 ozs. of spaghetti per person

4 rashers back bacon
4 eggs
4 medium sized onions

While you are cooking your spaghetti in the approved manner, peel and chop your onions finely and fry them to a light golden hue in a heavy frying pan with olive oil or butter;

when they are evenly coloured a pale gold, add your rashers cut into small pieces. By the time these are cooked your spaghetti should be ready for blanching and draining. When drained, add it to the bacon and onion in the pan, break the eggs on to the mixture, stir rapidly with a wooden spoon, and serve immediately the eggs have begun to thicken, a matter of a few seconds. Freshly ground black pepper is a necessary adjunct to this dish, as is a dish of freshly grated Parmesan cheese to be handed to the consumers and added to individual taste.

LASAGNE VERDI

These are the pale green strips of pasta, cut in oblongs as large as 3 inches by 2 inches, and although it is possible and permissible to use in their place the green ribbon noodles obtainable in most shops that sell pasta, you may, if you are successful with your home-made tagliatelle, wish to experiment with this refinement of pasta.

For six people the quantities are the same as those for tagliatelle, except that instead of lukewarm water for mixing, you need 3 ounces of puréed spinach (which is weighed after, not before cooking, remember).

Start again with your pound of flour heaped on a board, with a well made in the centre into which you break three eggs. After blending these with the flour, work in the spinach, and proceed with your kneading, rolling, drying and cutting as you did for the tagliatelle, except that instead of cutting the pasta into strips, you cut it into rather large, flat oblongs.

Using either your home-made oblongs of lasagne, or a pound of bought green noodles, you can make one of the most famous pasta dishes of all:

LASAGNE AL FORNO
TO SERVE 6

2 tablespoons olive oil
1 lb. minced beef
1 medium size onion, chopped finely
1 crushed clove of garlic
1 pint water
1 tablespoon tomato paste
1 lb. lasagne or green noodles
$\frac{3}{4}$ to 1 lb. Mozzarella or Bel Paese cheese
3 tablespoons grated Parmesan

Heat oil in a heavy frying pan, add the onion and garlic, and when slightly browned, add and brown the minced meat. Blend the tomato paste with a little water, pepper and salt, dilute with the balance of the water and pour slowly over the meat; cover and allow to simmer gently for 1½ hours.

Take 1 lb. lasagne and cook in rapidly boiling salted water, 5 to 7 minutes if the lasagne is home-made, 15 minutes if commercially packaged. Blanch and drain.

Grease an oven glass or earthenware casserole, and in it lay a layer of the cooked lasagne, a layer of meat sauce and a layer of Mozzarella or failing this of Bel Paese. Continue filling the dish in layers until all the ingredients are used up, finishing with the balance of the sauce poured over the finished dish, which should be topped with grated Parmesan. Bake for 20 minutes in medium oven.

LASAGNE IMBOTTITE
Stuffed Noodles
TO SERVE 4

- 1 medium sized tin tomatoes
- 4 tablespoons hot water
- 1 clove garlic, crushed
- salt and pepper to taste
- 6 tablespoons grated Parmesan
- 1 tablespoon tomato paste
- 2 tablespoons olive oil
- 1 stick celery, cut small
- 3/4 lb. cottage cheese
- 1/2 lb. Bel Paese
- 1/2 lb. sausages
- 3/4 lb. home-made lasagne or green bought noodles

Heat olive oil in heavy pan and brown garlic for about 3 minutes; blend the tomato paste with hot water, and add to garlic, together with diced celery and tomatoes; after about 3 minutes, lower heat and allow to simmer for one hour. Season with pepper and salt.

Fry sausage in separate pan until brown, and cut into small pieces.

Boil lasagne or noodles in boiling salted water as previously directed. Drain.

Into a greased casserole place alternate layers of lasagne, tomato sauce, Parmesan, more sauce, Bel Paese, sausage and more sauce, finishing with a layer of sauce topped with grated cheese. Bake in moderate oven 20 minutes. When serving hand at the same time balance of tomato sauce and grated Parmesan.

CANNELLONI FILLED WITH CHEESE AND SAUSAGE
TO SERVE 4

Although it is possible to buy the large 'channel' macaroni, and after a preliminary cooking to fill them with the filling mixture, the home-made variety is far preferable, and once again the recipe for pasta given under Tagliatelle may be used. But when it has had its final rolling it must be cut into oblongs about 4 inches by 3 inches, and cooked, a few at a time, in boiling salted water for four or five minutes, removed gently with a perforated spoon so as not to break them, and allowed to cool. For four people allow 20 to 24 cannelloni.

Filling:
3/4 lb. cottage cheese
grated Parmesan
1/2 lb. sausages
1/2 cup tomato sauce (see 'SAUCES')

Prick the sausages and place them in a pan, cover with water, heat and allow to cook until the water has evaporated, then let the sausages remain a few minutes in the fat that will have escaped from them in the cooking. Cool slightly, skin and mash the filling and mix with the cheese.

Place a little filling, about a tablespoonful, in the centre of each piece of pasta, and roll up into a tube. Grease a flat fireproof dish well and in it place the cannelloni side by side, and over them pour tomato sauce, not quite sufficient to cover them; dot with butter and sprinkle with grated Parmesan cheese, and place in moderate oven for 15 minutes before serving.

Ravioli & Gnocchi

Having mastered the cooking of pasta of the macaroni and spaghetti variety, let us now proceed to the more involved types known broadly as 'ravioli' and 'gnocchi.'

Both may be made at home, and after a little practice made well, and although it is possible to purchase both types ready-made and needing only to be heated and added to a sauce, if there is time available to make one's own ravioli or gnocchi, the results are well worth while.

Ravioli is the term loosely applied to the several varieties of little envelopes of paste filled with various forms of stuffing, and served either, like 'pasta asciutta', with a tomato or meat sauce, or, like 'pasta in brodo' in a clear consommé rather after the style of the Jewish 'kraplech', or the Chinese 'pork pellets'.

Once you have become expert in the art of making tagliatelle at home, you may, if you wish, use the same recipe for your ravioli, agnolotti, anolini, tortellini, or cappelletti, to give a few of the various names given to the many types of filled pasta. But when your paste has been rolled as thin as possible (remember, thin enough for you to be able to read the newspaper — or at least the headlines — through it), instead of rolling it into a roll as you have done when making tagliatelle, keep it in two large, flat sheets, or, supposing your pastry board is on the small size, a greater number of small sheets of thin pasta.

As each sheet is rolled to the desired thinness, spread it on a clean cloth, and keep it covered with another cloth, so as to prevent its going crusty and becoming too breakable to handle.

When your paste is made and the filling you intend using is prepared, spread a sheet of the paste on to a floured pastry board, and dot with the filling at regular intervals, say a teaspoonful of filling at intervals of about 1½ to 2 inches. Cover lightly with the second sheet of paste, after having brushed the 'walks' between the lines of filling with beaten egg to ensure that the second sheet of paste will close down over the filling. You may then either use a small round cutter, or, less wastefully, run a pastry wheel between the fillings so that you have a series of little filled envelopes of paste. Transfer these to a floured dish, being careful not to let them overlap, and cover with a floured cloth or paper until you are ready to cook them.

These can be made overnight if wished.

To cook, have ready a large pan of boiling salted water and transfer your envelopes of pasta one at a time, until all are in the water, allowing them to cook for four or five minutes or until they rise to the top of the pan. Remove them one at a time with a perforated spoon or slice, place in a heated dish, and serve with a generous helping of melted butter and grated Parmesan, or with any preferred sauce. These little filled envelopes are equally delicious served in a clear consommé, as one more form of pasta in brodo.

Another and slightly richer paste for ravioli and its kindred pastas can be made as follows:

- ¾ lb. flour
- 2 eggs
- 1 oz. butter
- ½ pint or slightly less warm water
- pinch salt

Sift flour and salt together. Place on a board and make a well into which break the eggs. When you have kneaded them into the flour, add the softened butter, and gradually sufficient lukewarm water to make a dough. Knead until smooth and easy to handle; cover and allow to stand for ten to fifteen minutes before dividing into two portions and rolling very thin on a lightly floured board, remembering to flour the paste lightly between each of its several rollings.

FILLINGS FOR RAVIOLI
Spinach filling

TO SERVE 6

- 1 cupful each of cooked puréed spinach and chopped chicken or veal (cooked)
- ½ cup breadcrumbs
- 4 tablespoons grated Parmesan cheese
- 2 eggs
- ½ clove garlic, if liked - crushed
- 1 heaped tablespoon finely chopped parsley
- salt and freshly ground black pepper

Mix dry ingredients and blend together with lightly beaten eggs.

Drop in teaspoonfuls at regular intervals on one sheet of pasta, cover with second sheet and press together gently around each mound of filling. Cut into squares with pastry cutter, and cook in boiling salted water in deep saucepan for 5 or 6 minutes, or until the envelopes of pasta rise to the top of the boiling water. Transfer carefully with perforated spoon to a hot dish, serve with Tomato Sauce (see under section for SAUCES) and when serving hand a bowl of freshly grated Parmesan cheese.

CHEESE FILLING
TO SERVE 6

5 ozs. each grated Parmesan and Gruyère
½ pint milk
2 eggs

pepper, salt, a pinch of nutmeg, and a pinch (fairly generous) of thyme

Blend well together, place in spoonfuls on a sheet of pasta as directed for previous recipe, cover with second sheet, press down, cut with pastry cutter and cook in boiling, salted water as previously directed.

When dished up, serve with melted butter and hand additional grated Parmesan to be added at will.

CREAM CHEESE FILLING
TO SERVE 6

1 lb. cottage cheese
4 ozs. grated Parmesan
1 whole egg and one egg yolk

2 tablespoons finely chopped parsley
freshly grated black pepper, salt and a pinch of nutmeg

Blend well together and use as a filling for ravioli.
Serve with melted butter.

MEAT FILLING
TO SERVE 6

- ½ lb. each raw minced beef and raw minced veal
- 2 tablespoons olive oil
- 1 oz. grated Parmesan
- 1 tablespoonful finely chopped parsley
- 1 egg
- 1 wineglassful cooking sherry, or preferably Marsala
- pepper and salt to taste
- a clove of crushed garlic if liked

Heat oil in a heavy pan, add garlic (if you are using), and chopped meat, and allow to cook for five or six minutes, add the wine, and cook for another twenty minutes; cool, and then add the beaten egg, Parmesan and seasonings; blend well, and use as a filling for ravioli, or for cappelletti (little hats), which latter are 2½-inch rounds of ravioli paste, in the centre of which is placed a teaspoonful of filling, after which the paste is folded over and sealed at the edges with a fork.

CHICKEN FILLING
TO SERVE 4

- ¼ lb. cold boiled chicken, chopped finely
- ¼ lb. finely chopped cold cooked veal or pork
- ½ lb. spinach, cooked and puréed
- 4 tablespoons breadcrumbs
- 2 tablespoons grated Parmesan
- 1 egg
- ½ clove crushed garlic, if liked
- salt and pepper to taste and a dash of nutmeg

Mix dry ingredients together, blend with the beaten egg and use as a fillings for ravioli.

CAPPELLETTI IN BRODO
'Little hats in soup'

Make cappelletti as just described, heat clear chicken broth to boiling point, drop in your 'little hats', and allow to cook for five to seven minutes before serving.

BACON AND SAUSAGE FILLING
TO SERVE 6

6 rashers lean bacon
½ lb. Mortadella
1 egg

pepper and salt
a pinch of nutmeg

Pass chopped bacon and sausage twice through mincer, blend with beaten egg, add seasonings and use to fill ravioli or cappelletti. This is an excellent filling for yet one more variety of pasta in brodo when cooked for five or six minutes in boiling clear soup.

Gnocchi

Although Gnocchi is placed at the end of the various forms of pasta, it is about the easiest form to make at home, for it requires neither rolling nor filling and consists merely of little rolls, croquettes or circles of pasta, various recipes for which follow.

POTATO GNOCCHI
TO SERVE 4

2 lbs. raw potatoes
½ lb. flour
2 eggs

½ oz. butter
salt and pepper to taste

Boil potatoes in salted water for 20 minutes, drain and mash with the butter; gradually incorporate the flour and beaten eggs and seasoning. Roll between floured hands into rolls the thickness of your finger and cut into pieces an inch long or slightly less. Have ready a pan of boiling salted water, and drop the gnocchi gently into the pan one by one, boiling for 3 or 4 minutes until they rise to the top — the water should boil only gently, not furiously. Transfer when cooked in a perforated spoon on to a heated greased fireproof dish, dot with butter and place in a warm oven long enough to allow the butter to melt. Serve plain, or with a meat or tomato sauce (see under 'SAUCES').

SEMOLINA GNOCCHI
TO SERVE 6

1¼ pints milk
yolks of 2 eggs
3 or 4 ozs. grated Parmesan

½ lb. semolina
1½ oz. butter
a pinch of nutmeg

Heat milk, and add semolina slowly, stirring constantly and cooking slowly until thick. Remove from fire, add beaten yolks of eggs, grated cheese and butter and seasonings and mix well. Rinse a flat dish with cold water and on it spread the semolina to a thickness of half an inch. Leave for an hour, and when cold, cut with a knife rinsed under the tap, into squares or diamonds 1½ inches or 2 inches across.

GNOCCHI ALLA ROMANA

Having prepared your gnocchi in accordance with the foregoing instructions, butter a fireproof dish and in it lay a layer of gnocchi, sprinkling with grated Parmesan and dotting with buter. Add a second and a third layer, with Parmesan and dots of butter between each, and to make dish attractive pile your layers in pyramid form. When the last of the gnocchi are used up, sprinkle with more Parmesan and over the whole pour 1½ ounces melted butter. Place dish in moderate oven for twenty minutes or until the gnocchi have taken on a golden colour. Serve in the dish in which they were cooked.

GNOCCHI WITH TOMATO SAUCE

As an alternative to the above dish, make your gnocchi about one quarter the size, and serve hot with tomato sauce just sufficient to surround each dumpling with sauce but not to have the dish 'swimming' in sauce. With these, hand a bowl of grated Parmesan cheese.

Rice

Although pasta, either pasta asciutta (pasta eaten with some form of sauce) or pasta in brodo (pasta in soup) appears with fair regularity in the Italian daily diet all over the peninsula, there is, in the north, a tendency to vary this by the use of rice dishes. Rice is cultivated in northern Italy on a heavy scale, and that grown in the Piedmont area, that is to say the stretch of country lying between the Bay of Genoa on the South and the Grain Alps of Switzerland on the North, produces a particularly fine, hard grain, equal in quality to the best that Patna in India can offer, and ideally suited to the long, slow cooking that is a feature of Italian rice dishes.

It is as well to remember to ask for Piedmont rice, or failing this to specify Patna rice, as the shorter, rounder grained rice, known to my local grocer as 'pudding rice', though excellent for that good old English standby, rice pudding, is apt to produce a somewhat sticky risotto. If, when shopping at a small local shop you are asked, as I have been asked: 'Do you want the pudding rice or THE OTHER KIND?' it's fairly safe to plump for THE OTHER KIND.

If you have never previously tried to cook a Risotto, the instructions may come as a slight bombshell, but I promise you, if you will follow them faithfully, the result will surpass anything you might achieve if you were to give in to the temptation to 'par-boil the rice first of all', to mention but one of the many incorrect methods. To all such suggestions I cannot too emphatically say 'DON'T'.

Supposing you are about to produce a risotto for four people, start operations a good three-quarters of an hour before the meal is scheduled — and just supposing you happen to be a working housewife, let me assure you that, heretical though the suggestion may appear to be, an excellent risotto can be prepared in the morning before you leave for the day's work, and re-heated so as to produce a really good dish for dinner the same evening — moreover, the flavour is apt to be all the richer if the various ingredients have had all day in which to insinuate their many and varied flavours into the finished dish. The one ingredient I prefer not to allow to remain all day in the risotto is the portion of chopped mushrooms, which, to my way of thinking, are much better sautéed in butter or oil and added to the dish not more than twenty minutes before serving time.

One thing to remember where the use of rice in Italy is concerned is that except in the case of the famous Osso Buchi, rice is not served with meats but whatever meat is used is mixed with the rice to form one integrated dish.

And now to your first risotto for four people.

PLAIN RISOTTO
TO SERVE 4

- 12 to 15 tablespoons Piedmont or Patna rice, the quantity depending on the appetites of the consumers
- 2 tablespoons best olive oil, or a mixture of oil and butter or, if you want it in the truly Milanese style, 2 ozs. of butter
- 2 medium sized onions chopped small
- 1½ pints or thereabouts of stock, chicken for preference, and if you want a touch of luxury, substitute a wineglassful of white wine for an equal quantity of stock
- saffron for colouring

Heat the oil or butter in a heavy pan, add the onion, chopped small, and allow to cook until it is a golden yellow but NOT brown. Add the rice DRY, and cook slowly together for a few minutes, stirring with a wooden spoon, until the grains are almost transparent. Now begin adding your stock — and now is a good moment to insert an asbestos mat between the pan and the direct heat of the stove. The stock is added in very small quantities a few tablespoonfuls at a time, and the Risotto is stirred frequently to prevent sticking. When the first instalment of the stock is absorbed, add the next and so on until the rice has finished cooking, and most if not all of the stock has been used. This should take from twenty-five to thirty minutes. Test the rice for tenderness towards the end of this time, and when it is tender and the dish looks creamy but is not sticky, the risotto is ready for the table. The grains, though tender, should still be separate.

To give your risotto a truly Milanese appearance it should be coloured a primrose yellow (rather than a buttercup yellow) with saffron at the end of the cooking time. If you are using the filaments — the dried stamens of the autumn crocus — take two or three of these, and having pounded them to a powder and allowed them to steep five minutes or so in a little warmed stock, strain and add them to the rice. You may, however, have purchased a thimbleful of already powdered saffron from an Italian provision shop, in which case add it, small pinch by small pinch, until the desired colour is obtained, but be careful not to overdo the pinches, as a little goes a long way.

This dish, omitting the white wine, is excellent with nothing added but a generous lump of butter and a few tablespoons of grated Parmesan, stirred in, allowed to melt and served immediately, before it has a chance to go stringy. With it hand more grated Parmesan to be added at will, and more butter, and you have a truly classic Risotto alla Milanese.

PLAIN RISOTTO

A somewhat richer version

Proceed as before, but with the addition of white wine, and if you can procure about an ounce of marrow from marrow bones, you will have a really rich dish.

You may also substitute for the white wine a glass of Marsala, but in this case I would advise against the marrow, as that and the Marsala combined would make the dish over-rich for most palates.

Now for the variations of this simple and typically Italian dish:

MUSHROOM RISOTTO
TO SERVE 2

- 1 rasher streaky bacon
- 2 ozs. butter
- 2 medium sized onions
- 6 ozs. rice
- ¾ lb. mushrooms
- 6 medium sized tomatoes
- ¾ pint stock
- pepper, salt, nutmeg
- 4 to 6 ozs. cold, lean meat
- 1 tablespoonful sultanas

Cut the bacon small and fry lightly in the butter, remove from pan, and add to the pan the chopped onions, frying them for two or three minutes. Add the rice and cook gently until it is transparent — about 5 minutes — add all the mushrooms except about two tablespoons of chopped mushrooms which will be useful for garnishing; add sliced and peeled tomatoes and replace bacon in pan. Add the stock in small instalments, giving the risotto a stir from time to time to prevent the rice sticking to the bottom of the pan. Ten minutes before serving, add the cold meat chopped small, and the sultanas, together with the remainder of the mushrooms which have been cut in small pieces and sautéed in a little butter. The rice should be cooked in about half an hour from the time it was added to the dish.

Serve, together with grated Parmesan to be added if liked.

MY OWN FAVOURITE RISOTTO
TO SERVE 4

12 tablespoons Piedmont rice
4 ozs. butter
2 medium sized onions chopped small
1½ pints stock
¼ lb. mushrooms chopped fine
½ lb. lean ham or gammon, cut into small pieces
1 cupful of cooked (or frozen) green peas
a few cooked French beans, if available
1 or 2 tomatoes, peeled and cut small
pepper and salt
a pinch of thyme
a pinch of nutmeg

Proceed as for plain risotto, but half-way through the cooking time add the mushrooms, which have been sautéed in butter, the ham, peas, beans and tomatoes, and the seasonings.

When serving, hand a bowl of freshly grated Parmesan, to be added at will.

RISOTTO WITH BRAINS
TO SERVE 4

¾ lb. lean veal
a little beef marrow, if available
12 tablespoons Piedmont rice
4 ozs. butter
1½ pints stock
4 tablespoons grated Parmesan
saffron to colour
1 calf's brain
1 medium sized onion
1 tablespoonful parsley
pepper and salt to taste

Wash the brains in salt and water, remove the skin and fibres and let them remain in salt and water till ready to use.

Heat butter in a heavy pan, add chopped onion and allow to cook a few minutes until the onion is golden yellow, add the chopped parsley, chopped veal and marrow if available, and allow to brown for 8 to 10 minutes; add the rice and the stock little by little. Drain the brains and cut into small pieces, and when the dish has been cooking for quarter of an hour or twenty minutes add these to the risotto and continue cooking until the rice is tender. Just before serving, add the seasonings and the grated Parmesan.

RISOTTO WITH SHELLFISH
TO SERVE 4

Make a perfectly plain risotto, but instead of stock made from meat or chicken, use fish stock if available, or failing this, plain water plus a wine-glassful of white wine.

Meanwhile, allowing five or six scampi or Dublin Bay prawns, or the equivalent quantity of lobster or peeled shrimps per person, sautée the shelled and cut up fish in a little butter to which a little crushed garlic has been added. Towards the end of the cooking of the risotto add the fish, together with the butter in which it has been cooked. Finally stir in butter and grated Parmesan.

CHICKEN RISOTTO
TO SERVE 4

If you have some left-over boiled chicken, remove any skin, and cut the meat into small pieces. You should have at least two breakfast cupfuls. In addition you will need:

1 medium sized onion	2 peeled tomatoes
1 clove garlic, crushed	1 small carrot
	1 stalk celery
¼ lb. mushrooms	2 tablespoons or thereabouts of chopped lean ham or gammom
¼ pint chicken stock; and later, when rice added, 1 pint more	
	1 wineglassful white wine
1 oz. butter	pepper and salt
chopped parsley	12 ozs. rice

Heat the butter and in it sauté the chopped onion, garlic, celery and chopped carrot; after five minutes add the chopped mushrooms, and the tomatoes cut small; allow to cook together for a couple of minutes, then stir in the chopped chicken and the wine and increase the heat so that the dish cooks fast for a couple of minutes more; add the seasonings; stir in the stock, cover the pan and allow to cook slowly for half an hour or so before adding the rice — 12 ozs. — and proceeding as for an ordinary risotto, using chicken stock or water for further moistening during the cooking of the rice.

Finally stir in grated Parmesan and a generous portion of butter.

RISOTTO GENOVESE
Rice in the Genoese style
TO SERVE 4

For this dish the rice is first of all par-boiled. Cook 12 ozs. of rice in boiling, salted water in a large pan as previously directed, but remove and drain a few minutes before it is completely cooked, and when drained, turn it into a clean saucepan, and to it add the following sauce, plus a generous lump of butter, cooking together and stirring to avoid sticking, for five minutes or until the rice has finished cooking.

When serving, hand with the dish a bowlful of freshly grated Parmesan cheese.

SAUCE

½ lb. raw lean meat, beef or veal for preference
2 or 3 stalks of celery, washed and cut fine
pepper and salt to taste
butter for sautéeing the vegetables and meat
2 or 3 carrots, washed and diced
1 medium onion, chopped
chopped parsley
a pinch of oregano or thyme
¼ pint of white wine

Heat the butter, and in it sautée the vegetables until they are a golden colour; add the meat and allow to brown, stirring so as to prevent sticking. Add the wine, and cook fairly rapidly until the liquid has diminished by half, then cover and simmer for an hour, by which time the sauce should have the consistency of syrup.

RICE AND PEAS AS SERVED IN VENICE
'Risi e bisi'
TO SERVE 6

3 lbs. peas weighed before shelling
1 lb. rice
2½ to 3 pints hot meat stock
1 tablespoon olive oil
1 tablespoon butter
1 tablespoon lard
2 tablespoons finely chopped parsley
2 spring onions

Shell and wash peas. Heat oil, butter and lard in heavy pan, add finely chopped onions and parsley and cook gently. Add peas and allow to cook long enough to absorb fat. Then add just enough hot meat stock to cover and allow to bubble before adding rice, having done which, add a further $\frac{3}{4}$ pint heated stock and cook gently without stirring for 25 or 30 minutes until rice is cooked. At end of cooking stir in a further tablespoonful of butter and 2 tablespoonfuls of grated Parmesan, and when serving, hand a dish of grated Parmesan so that more may be added if wished. This dish should not be allowed to become too dry in the cooking.

RICE WITH TURNIPS
Riso e rape

TO SERVE 6

12 ozs. peeled turnips
1 lb. rice
½ cupful tomato sauce (See 'SAUCES')

2½ to 3 pints meat stock
salt and pepper to taste

Cut the turnips in slices, spread on a plate, sprinkle with salt, cover with another plate and allow to stand for two hours, so as to draw off the surplus water from the vegetable. At the end of this time, drain the turnips, and place in a heavy pan in which you have heated the butter; allow to brown a little, stirring with a wooden spoon so that they do not stick to the bottom of the pan; stir in the tomato sauce and allow to cook for four or five minutes, then cover with heated stock, bring to the boil and add the rice. Cook gently for quarter of an hour or twenty minutes, adding more stock if the dish begins to appear dry. Do not overcook, or the flavour is diminished.

RICE WITH CABBAGE
Riso e cavoli
TO SERVE 6

Sufficient good hard cabbage to weigh ¾ lb. when the outside leaves and hard centre stalk have been removed

1 lb. rice
2½ to 3 pints stock, chicken stock for preference
salt and pepper to taste

Having removed the outer leaves and centre stalk of the cabbage, wash carefully, strain, and cut finely. Bring stock to the boil, add the cabbage, let it cook gently for five minutes, then add the rice and cook gently for a further fifteen or twenty minutes, or until the rice is 'al dente'. To give a richer flavour to this, try the addition of two or three slices of lean ham, finely chopped, and a little tomato paste 'broken down' with a few tablespoonsful of the hot broth.

RICE WITH CELERY
Riso e sedano

An agreeable dish is obtained by substituting for cabbage in the foregoing recipe a good head of celery, washed and chopped finely.

TO BOIL RICE

Now for a few comments on plain boiled rice.

You will need a large saucepan, with plenty of boiling water, and one or one-and-a-half tablespoons of rice per person. The saucepan must be large enough for the rice to move about freely while it is cooking, which allows surplus starch to escape into the boiling water, which is something it cannot do under crowded conditions.

Some cooks prefer to wash the rice before cooking, but actually, so long as it is looked over and any remaining husks removed, washing is not necessary as any dust there may be in the rice will rise to the top during the cooking and is easily skimmed off. However, if you are going to feel better about washed rice, by all means wash it.

When the water is boiling rapidly and salt has been added, add the rice and allow it to boil fast from fifteen to twenty minutes, depending on the quality of the rice and on personal taste. Towards the end of fifteen minutes test a few grains by biting, and when they are soft, and before they have had a chance to become 'mushy', remove the saucepan from the stove, and strain the rice through a fairly fine colander. Run cold water through the colander, shaking the rice as you do so to remove any starch still adhering, and then place the rice in a lidless, heated fireproof dish in a warm — NOT HOT — oven with the oven door left open, for a few minutes to dry. Alternatively, the drying can be achieved by placing the dish over a saucepan of boiling water on top of the stove for a minute or two.

BOILED RICE WITH BUTTER AND CHEESE
Riso in cagnoni

Allow a quarter of a pound of rice per person. Cook the rice as directed for Plain Boiled Rice, and when it has finished cooking and has been strained, place in a heated casserole, and add generous portions of butter and grated Parmesan, mixing well before serving.

As a variation, you may, if you wish, heat the butter first until it has become a golden liquid, and you may also, if you wish, flavour it with a little finely chopped garlic.

A simple dish by no means to be despised.

A RICHER WAY OF SERVING BOILED RICE
Risotto in cagnoni di magro
TO SERVE 4

Cook 1 lb. of rice in the approved fashion and when it has been cooked and drained, stir into it the following sauce:

1 onion chopped fine	1 tablespoonful chopped parsley
6 anchovies	½ cupful tomato sauce
4 tablespoonfuls oil	

Cook onion till yellow in the heated oil, stir in the parsley, and the anchovies, boned and cut into small pieces; cook together for five minutes, stir in tomato sauce, bring to boil and mix with the rice.

CHEESE RICE BALLS
TO SERVE 4

2 cupfuls left-over plain boiled rice	2 or three slices of lean ham, cut into strips
2 eggs	oil for frying
4 ozs. Mozzarella or Bel Paese cheese	1 further egg breadcrumbs

Mix together the rice and beaten eggs, and form into balls. Flatten each ball on the palm of your hand, and on the flattened surface lay a strip of ham and a strip of cheese. Close the ball together again, so that the rice conceals the contents. Continue till all the rice is used.

Finally dip the balls ('Suppli' if you want the Italian name) in egg breadcrumbs, and fry them in hot olive oil until they are a golden brown. Drain before serving.

ARANGINI
TO SERVE 4

Often when a train has stopped at a small station in Italy or Sicily, the attendant wheeling the 'Tavola Calda', the trolley containing hot food to be consumed on the train, makes his way down the platform to the accompaniment of the cry 'Arang-e-e-e-e-e-ni', and the hardy traveller who takes a chance on this typically Italian tit-bit is handed a piece of brown paper, containing a warm mound of rice, the colour of a pale orange, the best way of eating which is out of the paper, using the paper later as a napkin to wipe mouth and hands.

To make 8 of these 'delicacies', you will need the following ingredients:

1 lb. rice	¾ lb. lean minced beef
4 tablespoons grated Parmesan	2 tablespoons chopped parsley
1 beaten egg	2 hard boiled eggs (a refinement, this addition)
1 tablespoon olive oil	
black pepper	breadcrumbs and oil for deep frying
a pinch of salt	

Cook the rice in boiling, salted water, drain and mix with half the beaten egg. Heat the olive oil in a heavy pan, brown the minced meat in this, remove from the heat and mix with grated cheese, parsley and — if used — chopped hard boiled eggs.

Rinse the hands in cold water, take a handful of cooked rice, and in the centre of this place a generous portion of the foregoing mixture, closing the rice up to encase the mixture and form a ball. Repeat this until all the rice and all the filling is used up. Dip the balls in the balance of the beaten egg, coat with fine breadcrumbs and fry in deep, hot oil until they have taken on a light golden-brown colour.

A few left-over cooked spring peas are a welcome addition to the other ingredients.

The above recipe makes a delicious dish for home consumption, that is good eaten with hot tomato sauce, using any of the recipes under the heading 'SAUCES'. The railway station variety is rather less luxurious, and the hard boiled eggs are usually conspicuous by their absence, but nevertheless, it is tasty and filling on a long journey when there is no restaurant car on the train.

SARTÙ

Rice does not appear on the Neapolitan menu nearly as frequently as do the various types of pasta, but there is one rice dish that is a specialty of Naples, and that, in spite of the length of time required for its preparation, is well worth trying, particularly at a time when you have available some turkey or chicken giblets — why not serve such a dish on Boxing Day, as a change from the cold left-overs from the Christmas turkey? The list of ingredients, though formidable, is not necessarily difficult to cope with. For six people you will need the following:

- 12 ozs. of rice
- ½ lb. lean beef passed through the mincer
- 1 egg plus 1 egg yolk
- 1 clove garlic, crushed
- pepper and salt
- chopped parsley
- 2 one-inch slices of bread with the crusts removed
- flour
- oil or lard for frying
- about a cupful of cooked green peas
- ¼ lb. Bel Paese cheese
- ¼ lb. fresh mushrooms cut in small pieces or ½ oz. of dried mushrooms, reconstituted by soaking them in warm water for a few minutes
- turkey or chicken giblets, a small chopped onion, a little chopped carrot
- ½ lb. Italian sausage meat sauce with tomatoes (see 'SAUCES'
- about 5 tablespoons grated Parmesan
- crisp breadcrumbs

First of all, combine your minced lean beef, the bread — soaked in a little milk and squeezed dry — the garlic and chopped parsley with the beaten egg and egg yolk, together with the seasonings. Form into small balls or rissoles, and fry in hot oil until they are brown on both sides. Meanwhile, boil your rice in the approved fashion, in boiling, salted water and drain well. Cook the giblets with the exception of the liver, in a little water, with the chopped carrot and onion, for at least two hours, adding a bay leaf if the flavour is liked. Ten or fifteen minutes before the end of this time, add the liver and the sliced mushrooms. You are now ready to start composing your sartù. Butter a fireproof soufflé dish that is large enough to hold the combined ingredients, and after buttering it, sprinkle crisp breadcrumbs over the bottom and sides. Arrange about three-quarters of the boiled rice in a layer covering the bottom and the sides of the soufflé dish, and in this casing place the meat balls, the giblets cut into pieces, the mushrooms, peas and the sausages cut in pieces. Over this pour the gravy from the giblets and sufficient meat and tomato sauce to moisten. Cut the cheese in small pieces and arrange on top, and finally cover with the balance of the boiled rice, and pour over a little more of the meat and tomato sauce, so that the dish is moist but not 'mushy'. Sprinkle with a fairly heavy layer of crisp bread, crumbs and the grated Parmesan cheese. Bake in a moderate oven for half an hour. The ingredients suggested are, so to speak, the bare minimum, you may add to the glory and mystery of your sartù by varying the ingredients with a little chopped ham or breast of turkey or chicken cut small, and if you wish to be particularly luxurious, hard boil a couple of eggs, cut them in four lengthways and arrange them on the top of the dish before adding the final layer of rice.

FRIED RICE
TO SERVE 4

1 cupful left-over boiled rice
4 eggs scrambled
4 rashers streaky bacon
1 chopped onion
salt and pepper to taste

Cut bacon into inch-long pieces, and fry; chop onion, add to bacon and fry until it is golden; stir in the rice and fry till light brown, and at last minute stir in the scrambled eggs, and mix well.

RICE SOUFFLÉ WITH CHICKEN LIVERS
TO SERVE 6

- ½ lb. rice
- ¼ lb. butter
- ½ lb. chicken livers
- 4 eggs
- 2 pints chicken stock
- a wineglassful of Marsala
- 2 tablespoonsful grated Parmesan

Cook the rice for twenty minutes in the chicken stock, and at the end of that time stir in the cheese, butter and the chicken livers which have been cut in strips, floured lightly and fried in a little butter and the Marsala. Allow the mixture to cool, and then stir in the beaten yolks of the eggs and mix well. Beat the egg whites stiff, and fold into the mixture. Grease a soufflé dish that is large enough to hold the whole mixture, line it with buttered paper, and pour in your soufflé mixture, and cook in a moderate oven for about quarter of an hour.

RICE SOUFFLÉ WITH SHRIMPS
TO SERVE 6

Proceed as for the foregoing recipe, but substituting for the chicken broth either water in which fish has been boiled, or failing that, plain water; and for the chicken livers, half a pound of shelled shrimps or prawns.

Polenta

One more of the farinaceous foods beloved by Italians is the yellow maize flour, known as polenta, which can be obtained in Italian provision shops in this country. It can be bought either finely or coarsely ground, depending on the taste of the consumer.

It appears frequently on the tables of the north of Italy, frequently being used in lieu of bread, and although the plain boiled polenta is stodgy and uninteresting, if it is allowed to cool, it can be cut into slices, or formed into small dumplings, something after the style of gnocchi, and can form the basis of a good many agreeable dishes.

To cook sufficient polenta for four people, start off with six to eight ounces of the finely ground variety. Bring a pint of water to the boil in a fairly large saucepan, and to this add the polenta and cook slowly for about twenty minutes, stirring all the time. At the end of this time it should be thick and smooth.

Spread it on a large plate that has been rinsed with cold water, allow to cool, and then either cut it into slices, or with floured hands form it into little dumplings the size of a small egg.

The following are one or two ways in which the cooked product may be used.

BATUFFOLI AL SUGO
TO SERVE 4

Prepare half a pound of finely ground polenta as directed, and when cool form into little dumplings. Butter a fireproof dish, and in it lay a layer of these dumplings. When the first layer is completed, cover with a meat sauce and sprinkle generously with grated Parmesan, and on top place a second layer, continuing the layers until the dumplings are all used. Sprinkle little dabs of butter on the top layer, and a generous sprinkling of grated Parmesan; place in a hot oven for a few moments to allow the cheese to melt and serve very hot.

POLENTA AND CHEESE
TO SERVE 4 PEOPLE

Cook half a pound of Polenta as previously directed, spreading on a moistened dish or a marble slab to cool. Cut into slabs and lay these in a buttered fireproof dish, sprinkling generous helpings of grated Parmesan between the layers, and seasoning with salt and a little cayenne. Cover top layer grated cheese and a little butter, and bake in a hot oven until brown. Serve very hot.

POLENTA WITH TOMATO SAUCE
TO SERVE 4

- ½ pint hot water
- ½ pint milk
- ½ lb. finely ground polenta
- pepper and salt to taste
- 8 tablespoons grated Parmesan
- oil for frying
- 1 egg
- fine breadcrumbs

Cook the polenta for half an hour in a double boiler in the hot water and milk which have been mixed and brought to the boil. At the last minute stir in cheese and seasonings, and stir until thoroughly mixed. Spread on a moistened dish to cool.

Beat the egg and when the polenta is cold, cut into slices, dip in egg and breadcrumbs and fry in hot olive oil until brown. Serve hot with Tomato Sauce (See 'SAUCES').

If you don't object to the slight stodginess, you may eat your polenta as it comes out of the saucepan, hot, without first waiting for it to cool, with any of the meat or tomato sauces under the heading of 'SAUCES', or just with butter and cheese, but for the average English palate, the cooled and fried or baked variety is preferable.

There is a delicious sausage dish made with polenta that rather puts the 'Sausage Toad' of English war-time memories in the shade. For it you need half a pound of polenta cooked as directed in boiling, salted water; unsweetened tomato sauce (See 'SAUCES'), and a pound of Italian sausages, or failing these, chipolata.

Cut the sausages into 1 inch lengths, and fry until they are brown, then pour over them the Tomato Sauce and mix well together.

When the polenta is cooked, spread one half of it in a buttered fireproof dish, and over this pour one half of the sauce; add a second layer of polenta and the balance of the sauce. Sprinkle with grated Parmesan and place in a hot oven for a few moments so that the cheese melts and browns a trifle. Serve very hot.

CECI
Chick peas

These small, hard yellow dried peas simply MUST be soaked overnight, and after soaking they need long, slow cooking in salted water to which the addition of a half teaspoon of bicarbonate of soda to each quart of water helps in the tenderising process. Cooked in this way until tender, and cooled, they make a good addition to salad, seasoned with oil and vinegar or lemon juice.

CECI ALLA MARINARA
Chick peas, sailors' style
TO SERVE 4

1 lb. chick peas, prepared as suggested in the foregoing paragraph
pepper

2 or 3 tablespoons oil
4 anchovies
1 tablespoon chopped parsley

Having cooked the soaked peas till tender, allow them to keep hot in the water in which they have been cooked. Meanwhile, heat the oil, and to it add the anchovies cut small, the parsley and pepper to taste; mix well. Drain the 'ceci', and over them pour the prepared sauce, mixing well before serving.

Omelettes,
Egg & Cheese Dishes

If you are a lover of the light, fluffy omelette produced by the deft hands of the English or French omelette maker, you had better not order an omelette in Italy, for it is a heavier affair, it will be cooked in oil, and its filling, if it is a filled omelette, will be over-generous. If, however, you like your omelettes solid and substantial, you will be on safe ground.

Here is a typical Italian recipe for an omelette, which can be made 'asciutta' or 'morbida', that is to say, dry, or not so dry, and of the two, the latter more nearly resembles the omelette of France or England.

FRITTATA SEMPLICE
Plain Omelette
TO SERVE 3

Break six eggs into a basin, and beat them until well mixed but not frothy, adding a pinch of salt. Meanwhile in a heavy frying pan, preferably one kept only for the making of omelettes, heat 2 tablespoons of olive oil and cook over moderate heat, lifting the edges from time to time with a spatula so that the uncooked portion can reach the bottom of the pan and become cooked. Continue until there is no liquid remaining. Then, if you are an expert pancake tosser, and only then, toss the omelette so as to reverse it. If you are not so skilled, turn it with a metal slice and allow the other side to cook. Turn on to a heated dish and serve very hot.

So much for the FRITTATA ASCIUTTA, the dry omelette. If you prefer the more digestible FRITTATA MORBIDA, cook the omelette on the one side, lifting the edges so that the liquid portion may reach the bottom of the pan and become cooked; form it with the spatula into an oval shape, and without turning, slip it on to a heated oval dish and serve immediately.

OMELETTE WITH HERBS

Using the same basic recipe and procedure, try your omelette with the addition of a little chopped parsley, a little chopped basil or thyme, or a combination of several chopped herbs, and as an experiment, try the addition of a very little chopped rosemary.

FRITTATA AL TARTUFI

Again starting with the basic omelette recipe, before turning it into the frying pan, add a finely chopped black or white truffle.

FRITTATA AL FUNGHI
Omelette with mushrooms

While you are preparing the eggs, sauté a quarter of a pound of mushrooms cut in small pieces in a little butter and add to the omelette as it is beginning to cook, with a spatula fold the cooked portion over the mushrooms so that by the time the dish is completely cooked the filling is enveloped in the egg mixture, slide on to a heated oval platter and serve very hot.

FRITTATA ALLA SALSA DI POMIDORO
Omelette with tomato sauce

Before cooking, add two tablespoons of tomato sauce (See 'SAUCES') to the egg mixture.

FRITTATA AL FORMAGGIO
Cheese Omelette

To the basic egg mixture add an ounce of grated Parmesan cheese before starting the cooking process.

FRITTATA AL LEGUMI
Vegetable Omelette

If you have a cupful of cooked young green peas, or a similar amount of cooked asparagus tips, add these to the omelette as it is beginning to cook and proceed as suggested for FRITTATA AL FUNGHI.

FRITTATA AL PROSCIUTTO
Ham Omelette

Cut two or three thin slices of ham into small pieces, and add to the eggs before starting to cook; proceed as suggested for FRITTATA SEMPLICE. If liked, a little Italian salami may be substituted for the ham.

FRITTATA ALLA CIPOLLE
Onion Omelette

Chop a medium sized onion into small pieces and brown in a little butter; when cooked add to the basic egg mixture before starting to cook the omelette.

FRITTATA FARCITA
Stuffed omelette

Heat a little butter in a separate frying pan and in it combine ¾ lb. mushrooms cut in small pieces, a tablespoon finely chopped fresh parsley, salt and pepper to taste and a tablespoon of cream. Allow to cook together for five minutes. Meanwhile make an omelette as suggested for FRITTATA SEMPLICE, and when the underside is lightly cooked, pour on the sauce, and continue cooking, wrapping the egg mixture gradually around the filling. Serve very hot.

FRITTATA AL CARCIOFI
Artichoke omelette

For this the small globe artichokes which can be purchased preserved are used. The fresh vegetables are, of course, preferable, but are not always easy to obtain in this country. Take half a dozen of the artichokes, drain well, cut in pieces and fry lightly in a little butter, meanwhile preparing your FRITTATA SEMPLICE, and adding the artichokes as suggested for the sauce in FRITTATA FARCITA, just as the underside of the omelette is cooked, and wrapping the egg gradually around the artichokes so that by the time the omelette finishes cooking they are encased in it.

Now for a couple of really 'solid' omelettes.

FRITTATA DI PATATE
Potato omelette
TO SERVE 4

Boil four medium sized potatoes in salted water, and when cooked, drain and mash well, or pass through a ricer. Mix with the lightly beaten yolks of four eggs, and a tablespoonful of chopped parsley, and, if liked, a pinch of cinnamon; finally stir in the stiffly beaten whites of the eggs, and fry, first on one side and then on the other, in hot butter. Serve hot.

FRITTATA COL RISO
Rice omelette
TO SERVE 4

1 pint milk	3 oz. rice
4 eggs	2 oz. grated Parmesan
1 oz. butter	
salt to taste	a pinch of cinnamon

Heat the milk and rice in a double boiler and allow to cook gently until the rice is tender and the milk absorbed (about 1 hour or a little longer). Stir in the butter, grated cheese, cinnamon and salt, and when it has cooled somewhat, add the eggs, beaten lightly. Mix well, and fry in hot butter, first on one side and then on the other, or if preferred, bake in a buttered soufflé dish in a moderate oven till browned.

Solid, but satisfying, this one.

UOVE STRACCIATE AL FORMAGGIO
Scrambled eggs with cheese
TO SERVE 4

6 eggs	2 ozs. butter
1½ to 2 ozs. grated Parmesan	A little cream if available

Beat the eggs lightly, adding a tablespoonful of cream if available. Meanwhile warm the butter in a small stewpan, pour in the egg mixture, and cook over moderate heat, stirring continually, until the eggs are scrambled; at the last moment stir in the grated cheese and serve immediately on buttered toast.

UOVA COL RISO
Eggs with rice
TO SERVE 4

If you have a teacupful of cold boiled rice, this is a good way of using it up.

Allow two eggs per person, place them in boiling water and allow them to cook for not longer than five minutes, and as soon as they are sufficiently cool to handle, shell them. Meanwhile, prepare eight small ramekin dishes by greasing fairly liberally with butter, and placing a little rice in the bottom of each; place a shelled egg on top of the rice, and cover with a teaspoonful of grated Parmesan and dot with butter. They can then be 'poached', by placing the dishes in a shallow pan with hot water half way up the sides of the dishes, and cooking over moderate heat for about five minutes or until the cheese melts, or alternatively they may be baked in the oven for a similar length of time.

FRIED CHEESE

For each person allow two slices of Bel Paese about the size of half a slice of bread and cut very thin. Flour lightly, and dip first in beaten egg and then in breadcrumbs and fry golden brown, first on one side then on the other in hot butter, draining them after cooking so as to remove surplus fat. SERVE VERY HOT.

Fish

Have you ever stopped to consider the lack of imagination shown by the average — and I mean the average, not the exceptional — English housewife where the cooking and serving of fish are concerned? Yet look at our coastline, look at the variety of fish obtainable at most fishmongers' shops, and you'll probably agree that there's no real reason for our slavish adherence to...

> Boiled cod...
>
> Soused Herrings — delicious though they undoubtedly are...
>
> Fish'n chips...
>
> With crab or lobster, or a few shrimps or prawns for a special treat.

There's really no reason on earth why Friday, Fish Day, should not produce the tastiest and most exciting meals of the week. Take a look and see what our friends, the Italians, do about fish. To be sure, fish such as octopus and squid are not easily come by over here, and many of us wouldn't fancy eating them if they were, and for scampi we may have to make do with Dublin Bay prawns, but remembering the galaxy of fish now at our disposal, we can enlarge our repertoire of dishes very considerably. The following few recipes are offered in the hope that they will encourage experiments.

FISH FRIED IN THE SICILIAN WAY

Fry this now and again as an alternative to our own more conservative methods of cooking.

First prepare your fish by cleaning, washing and wiping dry, and finally dipping in flour.

Then in a heavy pan heat a good layer of good quality olive oil; when it is really hot, sprinkle generously with salt and when it is smoking put in your prepared fish, brown quickly on both sides, cover the pan, and lower the heat until the fish is cooked through. Serve very hot.

FISH AU GRATIN
Pesce gratinato
TO SERVE 6

- 6 ozs. rice
- 1 lb. floury potatoes
- 2 tablespoonsful flour
- $\frac{1}{4}$ pint milk
- 2 tablespoons grated Parmesan
- $\frac{1}{2}$ lb. butter
- $\frac{3}{4}$ lb. previously boiled fish, from which skin and bones have been removed
- breadcrumbs

Cook the rice as directed for 'BOILED RICE'; when cooked and drained, replace in saucepan, and mix with beaten egg yolk and 6 ozs. of butter, and allow to keep warm until the butter is absorbed. Meanwhile cook and mash the potatoes with a little butter.

Prepare a Béchamel sauce of 2 ozs. butter, 2 tablespoons flour and a quarter of a pint or slightly more of hot milk.

Flake the fish finely.

Having made these preparations, butter a fireproof dish and in it place the rice, forming a flat 'bed' on which to place the flaked fish. Form a border with the mashed potato; pour the Béchamel over the fish, and add a layer of Parmesan, grated and mixed with crisp breadcrumbs. Cook in a hot oven until the Parmesan has melted and the Béchamel has taken on a golden colour.

FISH CAKES
TO SERVE 4

about a cupful each of cold fish, and mashed potatoes	1 tablespoonful of chopped parsley 1 egg beaten pepper and salt

Flake the fish and combine with the potatoes, seasonings and egg; form into small cakes and fry until brown on both sides in hot butter or hot olive oil.

COD AU GRATIN

Allow one middle steak of cod per person and allow to marinate by laying it in a flat dish and covering with a wineglassful of oil, the juice of a lemon and pepper and salt to taste. After two hours drain, sprinkle with breadcrumbs and grill on a hot grill first on one side then on the other.

GRILLED SOLE

As with cod, allow your sole to marinate for two hours in a marinade composed of a wineglassful of oil, the juice of half a lemon — or a whole lemon if liked — pepper and salt to taste; drain, cover with breadcrumbs and grill on a hot grill.

In Tuscany there is a favourite fish dish, very rich, and extremely indigestible, but, having been warned, you may still wish to try it:

CACCIUCCO ALLA TOSCANA

This dish is interesting if an assortment of fish is used. Try the combination of sole with red mullet. Wash and clean your fish and wipe dry.

Meanwhile, in a stewpan heat a couple of tablespoonsful of olive oil and in it brown a chopped onion, a crushed clove of garlic and a little chopped parsley; add rather more than half a pound of fresh tomatoes, peeled and cut in small pieces, pepper and salt; when the tomatoes are cooked, add the juice of half a lemon, boil for a few minutes longer and then pass through a sieve or a food mill. Return the strained sauce to the stewpan, and in it cook your fish for half an hour or until tender; finally add a further tablespoonful of oil. Serve the fish on a heated dish with the sauce poured over and with it serve fingers of toast with which to soak up the sauce — you have been warned, this dish is rich, and somewhat indigestible.

ARAGOSTA LESSATA
Boiled lobster

You'll probably prefer to buy him ready boiled, but if you can bear to cope with the live beast, he's much better boiled at home. Place your lobster in a deep saucepan of boiling water, so that he is completely covered, and boil him for three quarters of an hour if he is a large fellow, half an hour for his smaller brother, and at the end of that time, if you are going to eat him hot, remove him from the water, rub the shell with a little olive oil to brighten the colour, and split him in two lengthways, and serve with olive oil, lemon and salt and pepper.

COLD LOBSTER

Allow your lobster to cool before cutting open lengthways, then crack the claws so that the meat may be extracted easily, and serve with a green salad dressed with oil and lemon juice.

FRIED LOBSTER

Having prepared your lobster, remove the meat from the body and the claws, dip them first in oil and then in flour seasoned with pepper and salt, or in a frying batter and fry in hot oil. Serve with sections of lemon.

CRAWFISH

These, known in some districts as 'lobster tails', may be substituted for lobster in any of the foregoing recipes.

SOFT SHELL CRABS

These are tiny crabs caught at a time when they are changing their shells, and they are considered a delicacy in early May in Venice. Minus their shells the crabs rise to the surface of the water and are caught in great quantities. The method is to flour them and fry them while still alive in boiling oil — delicious if you like them and can forget the wholesale murder that has taken place to provide you with your dainty dish.

CALAMARETTI

Again a dish met with along the Adriatic coast, where baby inkfish the size of large house spiders are fried whole in butter, often accompanied by scampi — truly worth trying and rather less off-putting than the soft shell crabs if you are of a squeamish nature.

If you are a lover of eels, here are a few typically Italian ways of preparing them.

ANGUILLA ALLA FERRARESE
Eels as served in Ferrara
TO SERVE 4

1½ lbs. eels, cleaned and cut in slices an inch thick
1 wineglassful white wine
1 bay leaf
salt and pepper
a pinch of mixed spice
a pinch of thyme
1 egg lightly beaten
breadcrumbs

Having prepared the eels, place in a casserole and over them pour the wine mixed with the spices and herbs, add the bay leaf. Cover and cook in a moderate oven for three quarters of an hour. At the end of that time, lift the eels from the sauce, drain, dip in oiled butter, then in beaten egg and breadcrumbs flavoured if liked with a little nutmeg, and fry brown on both sides in hot butter.

ROAST EELS

Large eels may be cut in thickish slices and cooked on a spit, with a bay leaf or two and a sprig of rosemary interspersed for flavour, and basted from time to time with olive oil and sprinkled with salt. Since we in England cannot often cook in this fashion, the next best thing is to lay the slices in a flat dish, and pour over them a wineglassful of olive oil seasoned with salt and pepper and the juice of half a lemon; allow them to remain in this marinade for at least an hour, turning them from time to time so that it may penetrate the fish, then place in an oiled fireproof dish, and bake in a hot oven till tender, basting from time to time with the marinade.

ROAST EELS
A variation

Instead of a bay leaf or two, use the same number of bruised leaves of sage, and so that the flavour may penetrate, lay the fish, when it comes to roasting it, on the sage leaves in an oiled fireproof dish.

STEWED EELS
TO SERVE 4

1½ lbs. eels
2 tablespoons oil
2 leaves of sage, chopped
1 clove of garlic

1 oz. butter
1 teaspoonful chopped parsley
1 wineglassful white wine

Skin and clean the eels and cut in pieces about 2 inches in length. Melt the oil and butter together in a stewpan, add the herbs, the garlic and the eels, and the wine; cover closely and cook over moderate heat for three quarters of an hour, adding a little water from time to time if it shows signs of drying up.

ARINGA ALLA GRATELLA
Grilled herrings
TO SERVE 4

8 medium sized herrings

a little milk

Clean the herrings and split them open, removing the backbone. Lay them in a flat dish and cover with a little milk and leave them to soak for a couple of hours. Drain; oil them lightly, and grill on a hot grill, serving them with sections of lemon.

MERLUZZO ALLA FIORENTINA
Cod, as cooked in Florence
TO SERVE 4

6 steaks of cod
salt and pepper
a wineglassful of white wine
a little chopped fennel
oil
flour

Oil a flat fireproof dish and in it place the lightly floured steaks of cod and over them pour a tablespoonful of olive oil, the fennel, pepper and salt and white wine and bake in a moderate oven for half an hour, basting at intervals with the sauce.

MERLUZZO IN SALSA
Cod with tomatoes
TO SERVE 4

6 steaks of cod
1 tablespoon olive oil
6 tomatoes, skinned and cut in pieces
1 small onion chopped

Heat the onion in a stewpan and in it brown the onion; add the tomato cut small and cook together for five minutes, add the fish, cover the pan and cook over moderate heat 30 minutes.

We in England are apt to turn up our noses at the grey slabs of salt cod we see hanging in a fishmonger's shop, but the Italian cook can teach us several good ways of serving this ill-favoured fish.

First of all it must be remembered that in order to render it acceptable at all it should be soaked for at least 24 hours, and if this can be done in running water, so much the better; failing that, change the water several times during the soaking process. At the end of the time, skin the fish, and remove the bones before starting any cooking experiments with it. In Italy it goes under two names, baccala and stoccafisso.

STOCCAFISSO IN SALSA
Salt cod in sauce
TO SERVE 4

- 2 lbs. of salt cod, soaked for at least 24 hours, skinned and boned
- 2 tablespoons olive oil
- 1 medium sized beetroot
- salt and pepper
- 1 medium onion chopped small
- 1 stalk of celery chopped
- 2 tablespoons tomato sauce

Heat the oil in a stewpan and in it brown the onion for a few minutes, then add the beetroot, washed and cut in cubes, the celery, the cod, cut in small pieces, the salt and pepper and cook very slowly for at least two hours; when the beetroot is tender, add the tomato sauce and from time to time add a little water if the dish shows signs of drying.

A variation

Using the preceding recipe, substitute for the tomato sauce a wineglassful of white wine.

STOCCAFISSO ALLA LIGURE
Salt cod as cooked in Liguria
TO SERVE 4

2 lbs. salt cod, soaked in water for at least 24 hours, skinned, boned and cut in small pieces

1 onion cut in small pieces	1 clove garlic, crushed
1 small carrot cut in cubes	1 stick celery cut small
1 tablespoon chopped parsley	2 anchovies cut small
pepper, salt and nutmeg	$\frac{1}{4}$ lb. fresh mushrooms
4 tomatoes, skinned and seeded	1 tablespoonful flour
1 tablespoonful olive oil	

Heat the oil in a stewpan, and in it cook the chopped vegetables and anchovies for a few minutes, sprinkle with the flour, and add slowly about half a pint of warm water, stirring constantly. Finally add the fish, cut small, cover the stewpan and cook slowly for two hours or a little longer, adding more water from time to time if the dish looks like becoming too dry.

CREAM OF BACCALA
Creamed salt cod
TO SERVE 4

2 lbs. of the best cut of salt cod, soaked 24 hours, skinned and boned and then steamed for $1\frac{1}{2}$ hours

Pound the fish in a mortar, adding a little olive oil from time to time and working till the whole is reduced to a creamy mass, adding, if it appears too dry, a little warm milk. At the end of the pounding, re-heat in a double boiler, then pile on a warmed dish and serve with slices of crisply fried bread.

POLPETTINE DI STOCCOFISSO
Rissoles of salt cod
TO SERVE 4

2 lbs. salt cod, prepared as for cream of baccala and allowed to cool	2 beaten eggs 1 tablespoonful chopped parsley a pinch of thyme

Mix well together and form into small flat rissoles. Fry in hot oil and serve with sections of lemon.

TUNNY FISH AS COOKED IN SICILY

For this dish the fresh tunny is needed, and the best cut is the stomach (ventresca), of which you should allow one thin slice per person.

Lay the slices in a flat dish and cover with a dressing composed of half a wineglassful of white wine, salt, pepper, a pinch of nutmeg and the juice of half a lemon, and allow them to remain in this dressing for two hours, turning them from time to time so that the dressing can penetrate well. Drain, sprinkle with a little chopped fresh rosemary and a little crushed garlic, and grill on both sides on a hot grill, basting it with the dressing. When it is nicely browned on both sides, decorate it with one or two anchovies cut in strips before sending it to the table.

TUNNY WITH PEAS

Again for this dish you need thin slices of fresh tunny, remembering that the 'ventresca' is the best cut. Brown on both sides in hot oil in a heavy pan, then add a medium sized onion chopped finely, and a teaspoonful of finely chopped fresh parsley, and cook all together for ten minutes. Meanwhile, partly cook some fresh green peas, allowing three or four ounces when shelled to each slice of tunny fish; drain and add to the pan in which the fish is cooking, add two tablespoonfuls of boiling water, and a similar quantity of tomato sauce (See 'SAUCES') for each slice of fish, cover and cook slowly for a further twenty minutes.

TUNNY AS COOKED IN LIGURIA
TO SERVE 4

1 lb. tunny 'ventresca' cut in thin slices
2 anchovies
½ oz. dried mushrooms, reconstituted by soaking in warm water for ten minutes
1 clove garlic, crushed
1 heaped tablespoonful chopped fresh parsley
2 tablespoonsful olive oil
½ pint white wine
1 tablespoonful flour

Heat the oil, add the flour, then slowly add the wine, the anchovies pounded to a paste and the other ingredients, except for the fish; allow to cook together for ten minutes, stirring frequently. Add the tunny fish, and pepper and salt to taste; cover the stewpan, and lower the heat, allowing to cook slowly for three quarters of an hour. Remove the fish to a hot dish, and to the sauce add a piece of butter the size of a walnut, and the juice of half a lemon; bring this to boiling point and pour over the fish and serve hot.

STURGEON, HOUSEWIFE STYLE
TO SERVE 4

1 lb. sturgeon cut into thin slices
1 chopped onion
1 tablespoonful chopped fresh parsley
salt and pepper
a pinch of nutmeg

2 slices bread, soaked in milk and squeezed dry
1 wineglassful of sherry
1 egg, beaten lightly
breadcrumbs for coating

Mix together the chopped onion, parsley, salt, pepper and soaked bread, and use as a filling between each two slices of the fish. Dip the 'sandwiches' in the beaten egg and then in breadcrumbs, and fry in hot butter, first on one side and then on the other, then pour over them the sherry, and allow to cook all together for quarter of an hour. Serve hot with the sauce poured over the slices of fish.

TRIGLIE ALLA LIVORNESE
Red mullet Leghorn style

Allow one medium-sized red mullet per person. Remove the inside, the fins and the scales and wash well. Lay the fish side by side in a flat dish in which you have prepared a 'soffritto' of a tablespoonful of olive oil, a clove of garlic crushed, a little chopped fennel, salt and pepper, and cook in a hot oven for ten minutes; then cover with tomato sauce (See 'SAUCES') lower the heat slightly and allow to finish cooking, for a further half hour in a moderate oven.

FRIED RED MULLET

- 1 medium sized fish per person
- 2 tablespoons olive oil
- pepper and salt to taste
- salted anchovies
- 1 clove garlic, crushed
- 1 tablespoon chopped parsley

Heat the oil, and in it fry the chopped anchovies, and allow the mullet to brown first on one side and then on the other; when brown, sprinkle over the fish the parsley and crushed garlic, lower the heat and allow to finish cooking — the mullet need about fifteen minutes cooking in all; just before removing from the fire, add a tablespoon of capers to the sauce and pour over the fish when serving.

TRIGLIE ALLA LIGURE
Red mullet as cooked in Liguria
TO SERVE 4

- 4 medium sized red mullet
- 1 tablespoon chopped parsley
- 2 anchovies cut in small pieces
- 1 tablespoonful olive oil
- $\frac{1}{2}$ pint tomato sauce
- 1 chopped onion
- a little chopped fennel
- $\frac{1}{2}$ oz. dried mushrooms reconstituted in warm water
- 1 wineglassful white wine

Heat the oil in a heavy pan and in it place the onion parsley, fennel and chopped mushrooms and anchovies, and allow to cook together for five minutes, then add the tomato sauce and white wine and cook for a further twenty minutes, stirring frequently. Meanwhile clean and prepare the fish and lay them side by side in a flat earthenware dish. When the sauce is cooked, pour over the fish, and place in a hot oven and cook for twenty minutes.

TRIGLIE ALLA TRIESTINA
Red Mullet as cooked in Trieste

TO SERVE 4

- 4 red mullet of medium size
- juice of half a lemon
- 1 wineglassful white wine
- 1 tablespoonful olive oil
- 1 tablespoonful chopped capers

Heat together in a heavy pan the oil, lemon juice, capers and wine, and after ten minutes add the cleaned fish and allow to cook for twenty minutes, turning the fish carefully at the end of half this time. Serve hot.

A GENOESE WAY OF COOKING FISH

This method may be used to advantage when cooking trout, carp, eels, mackerel, etc.

After preparing the fish for cooking, lay it in a stewpan, and cover with the following sauce, allowing it to cook gently for twenty minutes or half an hour or until tender.

SAUCE

- 1 tablespoon olive oil
- 1 chopped onion
- ½ wineglassful white wine
- ½ oz. dried mushrooms
- salt and pepper
- 2 ozs. butter
- 1 tablespoonful flour
- ½ pint water or fish stock
- 1 tablespoonful tomato sauce
- 1 or two anchovies cut small

Heat the oil and in it brown the onion. Then add the butter, and stir in the flour; slowly add the wine, water and tomato sauce, stirring all the time to make sure the mixture does not stick to the bottom of the pan; add the dried mushrooms, reconstituted in a little warm water and cut small, and the anchovies and seasonings. Cook together for ten minutes, then pass through a sieve, and use as suggested when cooking trout, carp, mackerel, etc. It is also good with cod fillets. Just before serving, remove the fish and keep hot, and add to the sauce the juice of half a lemon; cook the sauce for a further two or three minutes and when serving, pour over the cooked fish.

The fish section of an Italian cookery book would be far from complete if no reference were made to 'scampi', those natives of the waters of the Adriatic that, though they resemble our own Dublin Bay prawns, are plumper and have a somewhat finer flavour. Since it is not easy to obtain 'scampi' at one's local fishmongers, Dublin Bay prawns may be substituted, though with a wishful thought for the finer flavour the dish would have 'if only' one were on the shores of the Adriatic and able to obtain the right ingredient with ease.

FRIED SCAMPI

For this you may suit your own particular fancy; allowing ten or a dozen per person, remove the shells, and fry the fish in any of these three ways:

Dust lightly with flour and fry in hot olive oil, serving with sections of lemon.

Dip first in beaten egg and then in crisp breadcrumbs and fry in hot oil or hot butter and serve with sections of lemon.

Dip in a light frying batter and fry in hot butter, again serving with sections of lemon, or with Sauce Tartare (See 'SAUCES').

SCAMPI ALLA LOMBARDA
Scampi as cooked in Lombardy
TO SERVE 4

36 to 40 scampi or Dublin Bay prawns	4 cloves
	$\frac{1}{2}$ small onion, chopped small
1 wineglassful white wine vinegar	1 tablespoonful chopped parsley
1 bay leaf	a little chopped fennel
1 clove garlic crushed	salt to taste

Mix together all the ingredients except the fish, and cook together for five minutes in a stewpan; then add the fish, removed from shell, cover, and cook over a medium heat for quarter of an hour or twenty minutes, stirring from time to time. Serve very hot.

If liked, shrimps may be substituted for the scampi in the foregoing recipe.

SCAMPI ALLA MODENESE
Scampi as cooked in Modena
TO SERVE 4

36 to 40 scampi or Dublin Bay Prawns	1 small onion chopped fine
1 oz. butter	1 small carrot, diced
1 tablespoonful chopped parsley	1 wineglassful white wine
a little chopped thyme	1 wineglassful white vinegar

Heat the butter, add the other ingredients, with the exception of the fish and cook together for quarter of an hour. Meanwhile prepare the fish, add them to the sauce and cook over a moderate flame for a further quarter of an hour. Serve hot, covered with the sauce.

NASELLO CON PISELLI
Whiting with peas
TO SERVE 4

4 whiting
1 tablespoonful chopped parsley
1 lb. shelled green peas (weighed after shelling)
1 medium sized onion, chopped fine
1 tablespoonful oil
1 tablespoonful tomato conserve

Half cook the peas in boiling salted water and drain. Meanwhile, heat the oil in a stewpan, and in it brown the onion, parsley and the whiting; when the whiting is browned on both sides, add the drained peas, and the tomato conserve diluted with a little boiling water, and allow to cook for a further fifteen minutes over moderate heat.

CURLED WHITING

If you can persuade your fishmonger to prepare whiting in the old-fashioned way, skinning them and passing the tail through the eye sockets, allowing one per person, flour the fish lightly and fry a golden brown on both sides in hot butter in a heavy frying pan. Serve with sections of lemon.

PESCI ACCARTOCCIATI
Fish in paper cases

You will need pieces of greaseproof paper, one for each piece of fish to be cooked, and of a size large enough to envelop the fish entirely and wrap well over so that no juices escape. Oil the pieces of paper on one side, and oil whatever fish you are planning to cook, and lay it on the paper, after sprinkling it with salt and pepper, a little chopped onion, a scraping of garlic, chopped parsley or other herbs you may fancy, half a bay leaf, if you like the flavour. Close the paper by folding the edges together carefully so that the juices cannot escape, and cook in a moderate oven. The fish is served in its paper envelopes, so that each person may be served with the fish with the sauce unescaped.

This is an excellent method of cooking trout, steaks of salmon, steaks of turbot, cod or halibut, or whole prepared mackerel.

FISH TO BOIL

A wise precaution is to wrap fish intended for boiling in a piece of muslin; this prevents it breaking when it is removed from the saucepan in which it has boiled.

Allow ten minutes per pound.

Start your fish in cold water, in which you have placed three or four peppercorns, a bay leaf and either a tablespoonful of vinegar or the juice of half a lemon, and bring it to the boil quite slowly; once boiling, allow it to simmer for the required time.

FISH, TO ROAST

In a great many native Italian recipes you will notice the instruction to toast the fish 'allo spiedo' (on a spit), and since this is an implement not often to be found in the English kitchen, roasting in the oven has to be substituted. The oven should be hot, and the fish scored across with a knife and brushed with olive oil, and placed on an oiled grid in a baking dish or tin. Allow about ten minutes per pound and baste from time to time with oil and any juices that may have fallen into the roasting dish. Sprinkle with salt before serving.

OSTRICHE ALLA VENEZIANA
Oysters, Venetian style

At the risk of being accused of heresy for suggesting methods of cooking oysters, I would suggest trying this Venetian method.

Allow half a dozen oysters per person; open the fish, loosen them in their shells, and to each add a little of the following mixture, and a few drops of olive oil before grilling under a hot grill. Serve with sections of lemon.

MIXTURE

- 1 tablespoon chopped fresh parsley
- 1 stalk of celery chopped finely
- 1 clove of garlic, crushed
- a pinch of chopped fresh thyme
- pepper to taste
- 1 tablespoonful crisp breadcrumbs

PIGS IN BLANKETS

Oysters again, and oysters cooked. Allow six per person, remove from the shells, wrap each oyster in a strip of ham or streaky bacon, and fry in hot butter.

OR WITHOUT BLANKETS

Omitting the wrapping of ham or bacon, dip the shelled oysters first in beaten egg and then in breadcrumbs and fry in hot butter. Serve with sections of lemon.

FRITTO MISTO MARE
Mixed Fried Fish

If you go to Italy, and having visited a town on the coast come away without having eaten at least one dish of Fritto Misto Mare, then you might almost as well have stayed at home. In Venice you will probably be served with a mixture of tiny octopus, not much larger than a hefty house spider, scampi, and minute mullet, all dipped in a light batter and fried in hot oil, drained and served with sections of lemon.

Farther south you may meet some peculiar white circles in your Fritto Misto Mare that have a more than slight resemblance in texture to the pencil eraser of school days. Rubber it isn't, but ink-fish it is, and it should previously have undergone a fairly lengthy operation of skinning, having its insides removed, its eyes and ink-bag removed also, and the balance boiled until tender, and this may take up to an hour if you want to avoid that too-great resemblance to pencil eraser texture. When tender, and not before, the ink-fish should be cut into rings, and if you're frying your own Fritto Misto Mare, allow six of these per person, with the same number of scampi and one or two tiny mullet.

CLAMS OR MUSSELS COOKED WITH EGGS

Allow about 1½ pints of the fish per person.

Before cooking, leave them in slightly salted water for two hours so that they may open and the sand may come out of them.

Meanwhile prepare in a heavy pan a 'soffritto' of two tablespoonsful of oil in which you have browned a small chopped onion and a teaspoonful of chopped parsley; add the fish and, when they are opened, add the beaten yolks of two or three eggs, depending on the quantity of fish, and the juice of half a lemon. Stir the mixture, and keep it just below boiling point, and serve as soon as it is well mixed.

CLAMS or MUSSELS, FISHERMEN'S STYLE

Having cleaned the fish, place them in a covered pan over a fairly strong heat until they begin to open; uncover the pan at this point, and sprinkle the fish with chopped parsley and crushed garlic, and serve as soon as all are opened. You will find they make sufficient juice of their own not to require additional liquid.

SOLE WITH WHITE WINE

Allow one medium sized sole per person. Skin and remove the head and fins and dust with flour. Heat a little butter in a heavy pan until it bubbles, lay in the fish and cook first on one side then the other, then pour over it a wineglassful of white wine for each fish, and a little fish stock made from boiling together the head, skin and fins. Reduce the heat and cook gently until tender, by which time the sauce will have reduced in volume. When serving, strain the sauce over the fish.

The substitution of cider for white wine is well worth trying.

SOLE FRIED IN OIL

Allow one medium-sized fish per person; skin, remove head and fins. Dip first in flour and then in beaten egg, and fry quickly, first on one side then on the other, in hot oil until light golden brown. Serve very hot with sections of lemon.

PIKE
to be eaten cold

Prepare a good sized pike by scraping off the scales, removing the inside, and cutting off the fins. Tie in a cloth and place in a large saucepan or fish kettle with half a wineglassful of white wine, a wineglassful of water, a bay leaf, a pinch of thyme, a chopped carrot, a stalk of celery cut small, a tablespoonful of chopped parsley, a clove of garlic, two cloves and salt to taste. Bring to the boil and cook slowly, allowing ten to twelve minutes per pound. When cooked, allow to cool in its own broth, then strain and serve cold with a piquant sauce.

Or, if you like, to be eaten hot

When the fish is cooked, instead of allowing it to cool, lift from the fish kettle, remove the cloth in which it has been cooked, and serve immediately with any sauce you fancy, either a piquant sauce, or one of the tomato sauces (See 'SAUCES).

PIKE AU GRATIN

Clean a medium sized pike and allow to marinate in olive oil for half an hour or so. Sprinkle with salt and crisp breadcrumbs and grill on both sides until brown. Serve hot with sections of lemon.

TROUT or CARP

These when cleaned may be prepared in a similar manner and are excellent.

Many Italian cooks prepare fish and meats by cooking on a spit; since this is an implement rarely to be found in English kitchens, English cooks have to content themselves by using a grill where a 'spit' has been prescribed.

TENCH

Having cleaned your tench, allow to marinate for half an hour in olive oil to which has been added a little chopped fresh rosemary, pepper and salt. Drain and grill on both sides and serve very hot.

GRILLED GREY MULLET

Allow one medium sized grey mullet per person. Scrape off the scales with the back of a knife, clean and wipe dry. Oil all over and sprinkle with salt and pepper, and cook on a hot grill, first on one side then on the other.

RED MULLET

These should be eaten very fresh. Allow one per person. Scrape off the scales, and clean, removing all the inside except the liver; wash well, wipe dry, oil all over, sprinkle with pepper and salt and grill first on one side and then on the other and serve hot.

STURGEON

If you intend cooking a whole sturgeon, choose a fairly small fish. Scrape off the scales with the back of a knife, clean and remove the inside; wash and wipe dry. Make several small holes with the point of a knife and in these insert fillets of salted anchovy. Place in a vessel and cover with two wineglasses of oil, salt, and the juice of two lemons, a little chopped parsley and chopped thyme. Leave for 2 hours. Remove and drain; wrap in greaseproof paper and bake in a moderate oven for 1 hour; remove the paper and cook for a further 20 to 25 minutes, basting during this time with the mixture in which it was allowed to marinate Serve very hot.

ROAST TUNNY FISH

After our own brief acquaintance with beige-coloured tunny fish in small tins, it is a startling thing to behold one's first piece of 'tunny in the raw', a huge, liver-coloured piece of fish on a fishmonger's slab in Naples or the towns of Sicily.

For roast tunny take a fairly thick slice of fresh tunny and place it in an earthenware vessel with half a wineglassful of oil, some chopped parsley, chopped onion, the juice of a lemon, one or two cloves and salt and pepper to taste. Allow it to remain in this marinade for a couple of hours, turning from time to time. Drain, sprinkle with breadcrumbs and bake in the oven for 1 hour or a little longer, basting from time to time with the marinading mixture.

CAPPON MAGRO

If you are expecting guests for a buffet supper, and know them to be lovers of fish, you could prepare few things more appetising than this famous fish salad, originating in Genoa, but likely to be found in any seaside town in Italy. But be warned, it takes a lot of time for shopping, and for preparation, and it is costly. The recipe given below should prove sufficient for a party of eight or nine.

First of all, look out your handsomest round or oval serving dish, for this is a 'dressed up' dish. Next, if you want to do the job properly, procure half a pound of ships' biscuits, break them up, and soak them overnight in a tablespoonful of olive oil mixed with an equal quantity of vinegar. If you don't like the sound of the ships' biscuits, dry half a dozen slices of bread in the oven, and when they are crisp, treat them as suggested for the ships' biscuits. Next, prepare a selection of vegetables in season, say half a pound or more of small new potatoes, and similar quantities of shelled fresh green peas, French beans, young carrots, cauliflower; cook them separately in boiling, salted water — don't overcook — drain and set on one side. Prepare a head of celery, ½ a pound of button mushrooms, 2 ounces black olives, a similar quantity of green olives, and four hard boiled eggs; a small jar of preserved artichoke hearts would add interest to the dish; one or two small cooked beetroot would be colourful — and this is a dish where colour matters. Cut the mushrooms in pieces and marinate with a little oil and vinegar, pepper and salt.

Where fish is concerned, prepare a boiled lobster, ½ a pint of shrimps or prawns; half a dozen scallops; and two pounds of some good white fish, turbot, sole or halibut.

Poach the white fish and the scallops for seven minutes, lift from the water, flake and season with oil, lemon juice, pepper and salt. Shell the shrimps, and remove the lobster from its shell, and season these also with oil, lemon juice and pepper and salt.

Next prepare the special sauce for Cappon Magro:

1 teaspoon chopped parsley	1 clove garlic
6 anchovies	2 tablespoons capers
1 tablespoon chopped nuts	2 or 3 gherkins
a pinch of oregano	4 egg yolks (2 raw, 2 hard boiled)
¼ pint olive oil	2 tablespoons vinegar
1 tablespoon grated fennel root	6 green olives
	1 thick slice of bread, soaked in vinegar and squeezed dry

Place the parsley and garlic in a mortar and pound to a paste, add capers, olives (having removed the stones), gherkins, fennel, hard boiled egg yolks, bread, nuts and oregano; when all pounded to a paste, slowly add the oil, the vinegar and the two raw egg yolks, stirring with a wooden spoon; the finished sauce should have the consistency of mayonnaise.

All ingredients being now ready, you may start your dish. First of all arrange a platform of the ships' biscuits or bread, and on it spread a little of the sauce; next arrange the various ingredients attractively in pyramid fashion on the platform of ships' biscuits, a layer of flaked fish, a layer of assorted vegetables, a layer of the sauce and so on until all are used up. The bright-coloured vegetables, the sliced beetroot, peas and small or diced carrots, may be used as garnishes, as may a few unshelled prawns, the lobster claws, cracked for easy eating, and the quartered hard boiled eggs. This dish should, of course, be served very cold, and the 'prettier' it is in appearance the better.

Snails & Frogs

You probably won't fancy them, and in any case you probably won't be obtaining the live snails in this country, but just in case you want to know, you have to starve the creatures for a fortnight so that they lose all their slime and scum. During this time, to prevent their wandering, you have to keep them in a basket, wrapping them loosely in a cloth, which for hygienic reasons it will pay you to change fairly frequently. If you can stand this test of endurance, at the end of the time soak the snails in salted water with a dash of vinegar for three or four hours, washing them after that in running water until there is no trace left of the scum or slime. Boil them next in salted water for $1\frac{1}{2}$ hours, after which strain them and remove them from their shells, cutting away the black portion that you will find on the end of the body. After all this preparation, you may proceed to cook the snails as you fancy.

One good way of cooking them is to prepare fifty or sixty in the manner suggested, remembering that a dozen snails are none too many for a snail-fancier.

When the snails are finally prepared, place a tablespoonful of oil in a stewpan, allow it to heat and in it cook together for five minutes a crushed clove of garlic, a chopped medium-sized onion, a pinch of chopped fresh rosemary, and a teaspoonful of chopped parsley. At the end of this time add your shelled snails together with half an ounce of dried mushrooms that have been reconstituted in a little warm water and cut small, and two tablespoonful of tomato sauce; cook together for ten minutes, then add a wineglassful of white wine and allow to cook slowly for ten minutes longer, and serve hot — they're well worth all the trouble and fasting.

What with all this about frogs and snails, you'll probably expect 'puppy dogs' tails' to be included in the culinary catalogue, but disappointed though you may be, there is, to my knowledge, no recipe for these in the Italian repertoire.

Frogs, however, the Italian variety, make good eating. Try them fried.

Skin them, removing the head and the inside, cutting off the feet and washing them well, then leave them to soak in water to which a little salt has been added for two or three hours. Drain them and then cut in pieces and marinate them for an hour in a little oil to which you have added a chopped onion, a little parsley, a bay leaf, a little chopped thyme and/or rosemary, pepper and salt and the juice of half a lemon. Drain, and flour them lightly and fry in hot oil or butter.

Or for a more elaborate experiment try —

RANE ALLA GASTALDA

Prepare the frogs as suggested for fried frogs, but when they have soaked in water two or three hours, dry them, but do not cut them in pieces, truss them with the legs crossed over the body, flour them lightly, then brown them in a stewpan with a little butter flavoured with chopped parsley, a crushed clove of garlic, pepper and salt. When they are browned all over add half an ounce of dried mushrooms reconstituted in warm water and cut in pieces, and two wineglassfuls of white wine, and cook over moderate heat in a covered pan for half an hour or until they are tender. Serve with sections of lemon.

Meats

The following pages give but a small selection from the numerous ways Italian cooks have of cooking beef, veal, mutton, pork, and the various edible entrails classed in English butchers' shops as 'offal'.

To the casual visitor to the country, it might appear that no calf is allowed to grow to maturity, since 'vitello' (veal) makes so frequent an appearance on all menus, but living in the country one meets fairly frequently all the meats eaten in this country of ours, plus several unfamiliar to us, as, for example, young kid, which in taste greatly resembles lamb.

Sucking pig and equally youthful lambs are delicacies to be met with in Italy, and, despite their over-richness, they are delicious. Recipes for these have not been given, however, since they are so rarely met with nowadays in England.

MANZO IN UMIDO
Stewed Beef

2 or 3 lbs. stewing beef, NOT cut in pieces	1 onion
	2 sticks celery } all cut small
	1 carrot
2 slices streaky bacon	beef marrow if available
1 tablespoon tomato conserve diluted with a little broth	meat stock
	1 oz. butter

With the point of a sharp knife make several small holes in the piece of beef and into these stuff strips of streaky bacon; season with pepper, salt and nutmeg.

Having prepared your piece of meat in this fashion, place it in a stewpan with about an ounce of butter, a little beef marrow if available, and the chopped vegetables and allow to brown slowly, turning the meat so that it browns on all sides; then add meat stock nearly to cover it. Cover the stewpan and cook over slow heat for $2\frac{1}{2}$ or 3 hours. When half cooked, add the tomato conserve diluted with some of the broth, and continue cooking till the meat is tender, by which time the broth should be reduced in quantity and thickened. Serve in a dish, surrounded by the broth.

MANZO IN UMIDO ALLA TRIESTINA
Stewed beef as cooked in Trieste

a piece of lean stewing beef about 2 lbs. in weight	2 rashers of streaky bacon
3 cloves	1 onion, 2 stalks of celery and 1 carrot chopped small
salt and pepper	
1 oz. butter	
stock	white wine

Make holes in the beef with the point of a sharp knife and push strips of the streaky bacon into them; season with salt and pepper, and place in a stewpan with the butter, cloves and vegetables, and allow to brown; then cover with stock and white wine in the proportions of two to one, and cook slowly with the lid on the stewpan for 2½ or 3 hours, At the end of that time, remove the meat to a hot dish, skim the fat off the gravy and pour over the meat.

COSCIA DI MANZO ALLA CASALINGA
Rump steak housewife fashion

Take a piece of rump steak, and 'lard' it by pricking with the point of a sharp knife and pushing strips of fat bacon into the incisions; season with pepper, salt and nutmeg, and wrap in two or three slices of fat ham or bacon. Place in a casserole with a chopped onion, a cupful of meat stock and half a wineglassful of white wine and allow to cook slowly in a moderate oven for two and a half or three hours.

MANZO ALLA MASSAIA
Beef, domestic style

Cut two pounds of stewing beef into small pieces and place in a stewpan with a little olive oil, a chopped onion, a teaspoonful of chopped parsley and salt and pepper. Allow to brown a little then cover with stock or cold water and cook slowly for 2½ hours in a covered pan. An hour before serving time, by which time the broth will be somewhat reduced, make up to the original quantity by adding tomato sauce (See 'SAUCES').

STUFATO ALLA FIORENTINA
Stew as cooked in Florence

2 lbs. stewing beef cut in pieces for serving	1 teaspoonful chopped rosemary
2 tablespoonsful olive oil	½ wineglassful red wine
3 cloves of garlic, crushed	1 tablespoonful tomato conserve

Heat the oil and in it allow the garlic and rosemary to brown before adding the meat; allow the meat also to brown, then reduce heat and add ½ a wineglassful of red wine, and the tomato conserve diluted with a similar quantity of meat stock or water. Cover the pan and cook slowly for 2½ hours, adding more hot stock or boiling water from time to time if the meat looks like becoming dry.

If liked, potatoes peeled and cut in pieces may be added to the stewpan an hour before serving, so that they absorb the flavour of the meat as they cook.

Veal

Where veal is concerned, if you are able to buy it from a Continental butcher, do so, for you will find he has a better idea of cutting up veal for cutlets and escalopes than his British counterpart. Excellent veal can be procured in Soho from the shop of Benoit Bulcke in Old Compton Street, and there are other good Continental butchers to be found in other parts of London and in most large cities.

If you are buying veal for 'escalopes', you need thin slices of the lean meat cut from the leg or from the fillet, and if you are not the possessor of a 'cutlet bat', remember to ask your butcher to flatten the escalopes for you with his cleaver; this type of rough treatment means a far more tender finished dish, and an escalope, remember, should be tender enough almost to melt in the mouth when eaten.

It's as well to be extravagant when cooking veal, using butter for frying, rather than dripping; butter costs a little more, but the flavour is lighter and far more delicious when veal is fried crisp in good butter.

COSTOLETTE or SCALOPPE MILANESE

Either a cutlet or an escalope of veal may be cooked 'alla Milanese'. In either case allow one or one and a half per person, depending upon the size, and before starting to cook, either flatten the meat yourself with a cutlet bat, or have the butcher flatten it for you.

If you want to be truly Milanese, you will allow your meat to marinate in a bath of milk for an hour or so before starting to cook it, but this refinement may be omitted without any real detriment to the finished dish.

Remove all fat and gristle.

Coat your cutlets or escalopes in beaten egg which has been seasoned with salt and pepper; allow surplus egg to drip off, then dip the meat in fine toasted breadcrumbs before frying it on both sides in a generous amount of hot butter. Cook quickly on one side until golden, then turn and cook the other, and lift out of the pan with a perforated slice so that any surplus fat goes back into the pan. Serve with quartered lemons and a garnish of parsley.

You may either serve these hot, with a green salad, or having drained them well, and allowed them to cool, they are equally delicious served cold.

SCALOPPINE AL MARSALA

The combination of thin, crisply fried pieces of veal with Marsala is an experiment well worth trying.

Scaloppine, known sometimes by the name of 'piccate', are much smaller than escalopes; they are cut very thin and should not be much more than 2 inches square. Three or four per person is the usual allowance.

Beat your scaloppine flat, and flour them with flour that has been seasoned with pepper and salt. In a frying pan large enough to accommodate them, if possible, in one layer, heat a fairly generous knob of butter, and when it is really hot, brown the scaloppine very quickly on each side. While they are still in the pan, add about a tablespoonful of Marsala for every four scaloppine, and bring to a bubbling boil; add a teaspoonful of chicken stock for each tablespoonful of Marsala; stir well, and allow to cook for a few moments under a lower heat. Remember that one essential of this dish is QUICK cooking; altogether the process should take under ten minutes.

Serve very hot.

SCALOPPE ALLA MODENESE

Allow one or one and a half escalopes per person; flatten them with a cutlet bat, coat with egg and breadcrumbs and fry in hot butter. Then place the escalopes side by side in a flat fireproof dish, and on top of each place a slice of ham, and on top of that a thin slice of Gruyère cheese. Place in a hot oven, and serve immediately the cheese has melted.

SCALOPPE or COSTOLETTE DI VITELLO AL SUGO

Prepare your escalopes as for SCALOPPE ALLA MILANESE then arrange them in a flat fireproof dish, and over them pour hot tomato sauce (see 'SAUCES') which will be all the better if when making it you have added a bay leaf.

Serve hot, with a green salad.

VITELLO TONNATO
Veal with Tunny Fish

Remove the skin and fat from a piece of leg of veal; remove the bone, and stick the meat with small fillets of anchovy. Tie it firmly and allow it to boil for 1½ hours in a saucepan, covered completely with water in which have been placed a small onion, two cloves, a bay leaf, a little chopped celery, parsley and salt. At the end of this time, lift the meat from the water — reserving the broth to form the basis of a minestrone. Untie the meat, cut it in slices and place in a dish covered with the following sauce, in which it should be left for two days, after which it should be served cold, with the sauce served in a separate vessel.

SAUCE FOR VITELLO TONNATO

Mince the contents of a 4 oz. tin of tunny fish with two anchovies, and pass through a sieve or a food mill, adding olive oil and lemon juice in the proportions of three parts of oil to one of lemon juice, and finally adding a few chopped capers.

VITELLO IN UMIDO CON PISELLI
Veal stew with peas

- 2 lbs. lean veal
- meat stock and/or tomato sauce
- butter or oil for browning
- $\frac{1}{2}$ lb. fresh green peas (weighed after shelling)

Heat a little butter or oil in a stewpan, and in it brown the veal, which has been cut into 2-inch pieces. Add several tablespoonfuls of hot stock and/or tomato sauce (See 'SAUCES'), cover and cook gently for half an hour, adding a little more stock if it looks like drying out; add the peas, and simmer gently for a further $1\frac{1}{2}$ hours.

BRACIUOLE DI VITELLO ALLA VERONESE
Veal chops in the Veronese style

Allow one chop per person, and while these are being grilled, prepare the following sauce:

- 2 cloves of garlic
- 1 tablespoon chopped parsley
- 2 or 3 anchovies from which bones have been removed
- 2 ozs. butter

Pound together all the ingredients except the butter in a mortar until a paste is formed, then add the butter and cream well together. Pour into the dish in which the chops are to be served, and keep hot over a saucepan of boiling water. When the chops are cooked, arrange in the dish and serve hot with sections of lemon.

VITELLO IN FRICASSEA
Fricassée of veal

Cut lean veal into small pieces. Fry an onion until golden brown in a little butter; add the pieces of veal and brown on all sides; cover with boiling stock, lower the heat and allow to cook until about half the liquid is evaporated (about ½ an hour). Meanwhile, beat two or three egg yolks with the juice of half a lemon and a little chopped parsley, and when the veal has finished cooking, add the egg and lemon mixture, removing the stewpan from the heat so as not to curdle the eggs. Mix well and serve hot.

ROAST VEAL

Allow about 30 minutes to the pound at 300 degrees Fahrenheit. Pound together a clove of garlic and an anchovy, and rub these over the roast of veal before cooking. Cover the meat with strips of fat bacon or salt pork to prevent its drying out, and cook in a casserole with a little butter. Be careful if you are salting it not to overdo this, as the anchovy will have made it fairly salty. At the end of the cooking, add a half a glass of red wine to the gravy, and baste the veal with this before removing from the oven.

OSSOBUCO

This is the knuckle of veal, rich and tasty when prepared 'Alla Milanese'.

OSSOBUCO ALLA MILANESE
TO SERVE 4

Allow one small knuckle of veal per person, and it should be sawn nearly through in sections about 1½ or 2 inches long, so that one has a number of sections of bone, each surrounded by a circle of muscle.

2 or 3 ozs. butter
flour
salt and pepper
1 wineglassful dry white wine
1 tablespoonful chopped parsley
1 anchovy
grated rind of half a lemon
stock or water

Heat the butter in a heavy pan large enough to accommodate the veal knuckles in one layer; flour the knuckles and brown on both sides in the hot butter, seasoning with salt and pepper; add the wine, and continue cooking until the wine has almost evaporated, then add stock or water just to cover the meat; cover closely, and cook slowly for at least an hour, adding more stock if it looks as though the meat is drying. Meanwhile pound together in a mortar the garlic, anchovy, lemon rind and parsley, and five minutes before serving, add to the gravy, and bring to the boil, stirring with a wooden spoon.

It is customary to serve Ossobuco with a plain Risotto, coloured with saffron; this, incidentally, is the only instance of rice served *with* a meat dish.

AGNELLO ARROSTO
Roast Lamb

Try roasting a leg of lamb Italian fashion. Before putting it in the oven, make a slit in the flesh near the bone and into this place one or two cloves of garlic and a sprig of rosemary. Oil the meat lightly all over, and place in a hot oven, allowing 15 minutes to the pound and 15 minutes over, and basting from time to time with oil, and, to make it even more delicious, 15 minutes before serving, pour over it a wineglassful of white wine and baste finally with the juices that have run into the roasting pan.

AGNELLO O CAPRETTO IN CASSERUOLA
Lamb or Kid Pot Roast

Kid is eaten a great deal in Italy and the flesh of young goats makes excellent eating. Try a leg of either kid or lamb stuck at intervals with rosemary, salted, and then browned on all sides in a stewpan in which two tablespoonsful of olive oil have been heated. Cover the stewpan when the flesh is browned on all sides, and allow it to cook slowly, 15 minutes to the pound, in the steam that will develop in the stewpan once it is covered.

PORK COOKED IN MILK 'ALLA BOLOGNESE'

For this you need a piece of loin of pork, boned and with some of its fat removed. If you are going to cook it in the true Bolognese manner, you will prepare it overnight by sprinkling with salt and pepper and leaving till morning, but this treatment is not absolutely essential if time is at a premium.

If you are preparing the meat the day you are cooking, sprinkle it with salt and black pepper before rolling it up, and it is an improvement if a clove of garlic is sliced thin and rolled up in the centre of the meat, together with a few seeds of coriander or fennel.

Use a saucepan that is more or less the size of the rolled joint, and when the pork is ready for the pan, heat a little butter in it and brown the pork all over.

Heat the milk, allowing roughly a pint of milk to each pound of pork, and pour over the meat. Cover the saucepan and allow to simmer gently for an hour or a little longer; uncover, and allow to cook for another half hour, by which time the quantity of liquid will be reduced considerably, and it should be a golden brown in colour. Take care that the saucepan does not go dry; if there is any danger of this, add a little more hot milk.

The joint is excellent hot, served with the sauce from the cooking, and if you are able to add a few sliced truffles to this it is all the better.

Another addition is that of a chopped onion and a rasher of bacon cut in small pieces, and cooked in the butter before the pork is browned.

LOIN OF PORK
as cooked in Tuscany

Again your loin pork should be boned and some of its fat should be removed before cooking, and before rolling it should be stuck with a few rosemary leaves and a few slivers of garlic, and seasoned with salt and pepper. Roll and tie it and roast in the oven in the usual fashion, allowing 25 to 30 minutes per pound, plus 25 or 30 minutes over. This is excellent allowed to cool and served with a potato salad.

And as cooked in Perugia

Here, instead of rosemary, fennel leaves are used, and when the meat is cooked and served cold, it is a good touch to serve with it a potato salad with which has been mixed a little thinly sliced fennel.

PORK CHOPS
'ALLA NAPOLITANA'
TO SERVE 6

The Neapolitans use a lot of green and red and yellow peppers in their cooking, and these 'marry' well with pork. For this recipe take:

- 6 pork chops
- 2 red or yellow peppers
- ½ lb. mushrooms
- 1 tablespoonful tomato paste
- oil for cooking
- salt and pepper
- 1 clove of garlic, crushed

Heat oil in a heavy pan, fry garlic in it till pale brown, add the chops and brown on both sides; add salt and pepper. Remove from the pan and keep warm. Meanwhile, dilute the tomato paste with a little water and add to the pan in which the chops have been cooked, remove the seeds and stem from the peppers and chop them finely, and add these to the pan together with the chopped mushrooms; cover and cook slowly for about quarter of an hour, then replace the chops, cooking together for another twenty minutes or so. Serve very hot.

PORK CHOPS WITH PRUNES
TO SERVE 6

6 pork chops
salt and pepper

oil or butter for frying
2 tablespoons white wine

Heat the oil with the pepper and salt in a stewpan and in it fry the chops first on one side and then on the other until brown, add the wine and cook over slightly lowered heat until the wine has evaporated, then remove the chops to a hot dish and cover with the following sauce.

SAUCE

1 onion
1 oz. butter
10 or a dozen prunes which have been soaked in water until softened

2 slices lean ham
2 tablespoons wine vinegar
salt
chopped thyme
bay leaf

Soak the prunes, and when soft remove the stones. Fry the chopped onion and ham cut in small pieces in butter until light brown, add the vinegar, and cook until the sauce is reduced by one-half. Place the prunes in a small saucepan, with barely enough water to cover them, a pinch of chopped thyme and a bay leaf and cook slowly till soft. Pass through a sieve or food mill and add to the chopped onion and ham; mix well and pour over the pork chops.

SALSICCIE ALLA TRIESTINA
Sausages as cooked in Trieste
TO SERVE 4

1 lb. pure pork sausages	2 tablespoons grated Parmesan
1 wineglassful white wine	meat stock

Puncture the sausages, then place in a saucepan with a few tablespoons of stock, and a wineglassful of white wine and cook gently on the top of the stove for about twenty minutes; at the end of that time, add the Parmesan cheese, stir well, and serve very hot.

SAUSAGES WITH TOMATO SAUCE
TO SERVE 4

1 lb. pure pork sausages	chopped sage
olive oil	tomato sauce (See 'SAUCES')

Puncture the sausages, then fry in the olive oil to which a teaspoonful of chopped sage has been added; when they are browned, cover with tomato sauce. Cover pan and cook gently for twenty minutes. The sage may be omitted if the flavour is not liked.

FEGATO ALLA SPAGNOLA
Liver as served in Spain
TO SERVE 6

1½ lbs. calf's liver	1 dozen small firm tomatoes
2 large onions sliced thinly into rings	1 lemon
sprigs of parsley	oil
flour	salt and pepper

Heat the grill, and meanwhile, dip the liver — sliced to about the thickness of half an inch — in the flour, then into oil, and grill first on one side then on the other. Set on one side to keep warm, and having seasoned the tomatoes with salt, pepper and oil, grill these also. While this is going on, fry the onions until a golden yellow. Have ready a large flat dish, and pile the onions into a pyramid in the centre, with the slices of liver around, garnished with grilled tomatoes and sprigs of parsley, and the lemon cut into sections.

FEGATO ALL' ITALIANA
Liver in the Italian style
TO SERVE 6

1½ lbs. calf's liver, cut into thin slices	flour pepper and salt 1 lemon
2 ozs. butter	

Heat the butter very hot in a large heavy frying pan. Flour the slices of liver and fry quickly, first on one side and then on the other, the whole process to take not more than five or six minutes. Season with pepper and salt, add a small knob of butter, and shake the pan well so that it is distributed over the slices of liver. Remove the pan from the fire, and sprinkle the liver with the juice of half a lemon before removing to a hot dish for serving. Serve very hot.

Having tried out these two fairly conservative methods of cooking liver, how about trying a Tuscan specialty, as per the following recipe:

FEGATO ALLA TOSCANA
TO SERVE 6

1½ lbs. calf's liver cut into thin slices	a good tablespoonful of fresh sage leaves chopped small
flour	
oil	1 lemon, cut into sections
pepper and salt	

Flour the liver, and fry in hot oil very quickly; before removing from the stove, season with pepper and salt, and the sage leaves cut small. Serve very hot accompanied by sections of lemon.

Or, having enjoyed veal escalopes alla Milanese, why not try liver treated similarly?

FEGATO ALLA MILANESE
TO SERVE 6

1½ lbs. calf's liver, cut into thin slices	1 beaten egg
flour	breadcrumbs
pepper and salt	butter for frying
a tablespoon chopped parsley	1 lemon

For this recipe, start preparations an hour and a quarter before you wish to serve the dish, for the slices of liver are spread on a flat dish, seasoned with salt, pepper and the chopped parsley and left to 'mind their own business' for a good hour. At the end of this time, heat the butter in a heavy pan; flour the liver, then dip in beaten egg, and then into crisp breadcrumbs, and fry quickly first on one side and then on the other. Arrange on a flat, heated dish, pour over the liver the remainder of the butter in which it was fried, and garnish with sections of lemon and sprigs of parsley.

While in Venice the method is strongly reminiscent of 'liver and onions', except that oil is used for cooking whereas we normally use lard or dripping:

FEGATO ALLA VENEZIANA

For each person allow about a quarter of a pound of liver and one large onion cut into rings. Heat the oil in a heavy pan and in it cook the onions until they are a golden yellow; add the liver — floured — and cook quickly on either side, season with salt and pepper and serve piled upon a bed of the fried onions.

Then, for real luxury, why not try liver cooked with artichokes? Since 'Globe' artichokes are not always easy to obtain in this country, you may have to make do with the bottled or tinned variety, well drained.

LIVER WITH ARTICHOKES

For each person allow quarter of a pound of calf's liver, and one or two artichokes.

In a heavy pan fry a chopped onion in a little oil until it is golden brown; lower the heat and add the artichokes divided into sections, and cook slowly for twenty minutes or so until the artichokes are tender; increase the heat, add the floured liver and cook quickly on first one side then the other; remove from the heat, season with salt, pepper and a tablespoonful of finely chopped parsley; sprinkle with lemon juice, and shake the pan well so that liver and artichokes are impregnated with the seasonings and lemon juice. Serve on a hot dish.

Here is an excellent way of serving pig's liver as prepared in Tuscany. There it is customary to serve the liver thus treated on a skewer, interspersed with small sections of toast, and bay leaves, but since grilling on a skewer is not the easiest way of cooking with modern appliances, omit the toast and the bay leaves, and having dipped your thin slices of pig's liver in beaten egg, dip them in the following mixture so that they are completely coated with it, and fry quickly in hot oil, then serve with sections of lemon.

MIXTURE FOR COATING

A good handful of crisp breadcrumbs; a clove of garlic, crushed or cut very fine, a teaspoonful of fennel seeds, salt and pepper. Mix well together and when the liver has been dipped in beaten egg, coat with this mixture before frying in hot oil.

FLAN DI FEGATO

½ lb. calves' liver or chicken livers
1 slice ham
a pinch of spices
2 slices of bread soaked in stock and squeezed dry
1 oz. butter
2 ozs. salt pork
1 or 2 truffles or ½ oz. dried mushrooms (soaked in water for ten minutes)

Pass all ingredients through a mincer and add half a wineglassful of Marsala, half a wineglassful of stock, two whole eggs and one additional yolk; mix well and place in a greased soufflé dish and cook in a moderate oven for twenty minutes or half an hour.

POLPETTE DI FEGATO
Liver rissoles

½ lb. calves' liver
1 slice fat pork
2 slices bread soaked in stock and squeezed dry

Pound these to a pulp with a pestle and mortar, then add three tablespoons grated Parmesan cheese, salt and pepper to taste, two egg yolks beaten, and form into small rissoles the size of a walnut. Sprinkle with flour and fry in a 'soffrito' of oil and chopped onion. Sprinkle with a little white wine when they are half cooked.

TRIPPA ALL'ITALIANA
Tripe, Italian fashion
TO SERVE 4

1 lb. tripe	1 large onion
1 clove garlic	4 tablespoons olive
1 dessertspoon	oil
flour	2 medium tomatoes,
1 pint stock	peeled
1 teaspoon chopped	1 carrot
basil	1 stalk celery
salt	1 teaspoon
bay leaf	chopped parsley
pepper	

Heat the oil and in it fry the chopped onion and crushed garlic until they are golden brown and then stir in the flour. Cut the washed tripe into squares, and add to the mixture together with the tomatoes peeled and cut small. Slowly add the stock, stirring to prevent sticking to bottom of pan; add diced celery and carrot and seasoning. Allow to simmer gently for an hour and a half. Serve hot, removing the bay leaf before serving.

TRIPPA ALLA FIORENTINA
Tripe, Florentine style
TO SERVE 4

1 lb. tripe	½ pint tomato sauce
pepper and salt,	(See 'SAUCES')
to taste	1 teaspoon chopped
2 tablespoons Par-	marjoram
mesan cheese	

Cut the tripe into squares and boil for half an hour in boiling, salted water. Drain; then place in a stewpan with the tomato sauce and allow to simmer gently for a further hour; a quarter of an hour before serving, sprinkle in the marjoram, and when dished up, scatter the grated cheese over it, or hand it in a separate dish to be added at will.

TRIPE WITH PARMESAN
TO SERVE 4

1 lb. tripe
2 ozs. butter

3 tablespoons Parmesan cheese grated

Cut the tripe into small squares and cook in boiling, salted water for an hour and a half or until tender; drain, and reheat with the butter. When hot, stir in the Parmesan cheese and serve as soon as this starts to melt.

ROGNONI IN UMIDO
Stewed kidneys
TO SERVE 4

1 lb. calves' or sheep's kidneys
1½ oz. butter
2 wineglassesful white wine

1 teaspoonful chopped parsley
half a lemon
1 small onion

The kidneys must be skinned, cut in halves and the core removed; after this plunge them in boiling water to which juice of the half lemon has been added. After two or three minutes, drain them and cut in slices. Heat the butter in a stewpan, and in it cook the chopped onion until light brown, add the kidneys and cook them for five or six minutes, shaking the pan from time to time to prevent sticking, add the wine and a little grated lemon rind, and allow the dish to bubble so that the gravy is reduced in volume; finally, a few minutes before serving, add the parsley. Serve hot in a dish surrounded by snippets of toast.

ROGNONI ALLA BOLOGNESE
Kidneys as cooked in Bologna
TO SERVE 4

1 lb. calves' or pigs' kidneys
2 ozs. butter
juice of half a lemon
2 medium sized onions
¼ pint stock
1 tablespoon chopped parsley

Skin the kidneys, cut in half, removing the core, then plunge in boiling water to which a little vinegar or lemon juice has been added and leave for two or three minutes. Drain and cut in slices. Heat the butter in a stewpan and in it fry the chopped onion until golden brown and add the parsley; add the chopped kidneys and cook for five or six minutes, shaking the pan so that they are cooked on all sides and do not stick; finally, add the stock and a little lemon juice and cook gently for a further 10 minutes, but do not allow to boil.

TESTA DI VITELLO ALLA TOSCANA
Brains as cooked in Tuscany
TO SERVE 4

Calves' brains
1 oz. butter
1 small onion
1 tablespoon parsley, chopped
juice of half a lemon
1 carrot
1 stalk celery
salt and pepper

Wash the brains in salt and water, removing the skin and fibres and allow to remain in salt and water for half an hour or longer. Wrap in a piece of muslin and tie with string and put on to cook in a stewpan with water to cover and the chopped vegetables, seasoning and lemon juice, and cook for a further 15 or 20 minutes, or until the brains are firm; remove from the stewpan, untie, and serve on a hot dish with a piquant sauce.

BRAIN RISSOLES

brains prepared as for TESTA DI VITELLO
    ALLA TOSCANA
beaten egg   pepper and salt

Having prepared the brains as in the foregoing recipe, allow to cook and then chop fine and bind together with the beaten egg; stir over the fire in a small pan until the mixture thickens but does not boil; allow to cook and then form into small rissoles, which fry in hot oil or butter after coating with egg and fine breadcrumbs. Serve with sections of lemon.

LINGUA ALLA SALSA
Tongue with sauce
TO SERVE 8

1 calf's tongue	1 medium sized onion
1 lb. rump steak	
1 teaspoon chopped basil	1 teaspoon chopped parsley
½ pint stock	1 bay leaf
2 slices streaky bacon	¼ lb. mushrooms
	salt and pepper

Put the tongue in a stewpan with salted water to cover and bring to the boil, then simmer gently for at least 1½ hours. Drain, cool and remove the skin; puncture it here and there and into the holes introduce slivers of the streaky bacon. Grease a stewpan and in it place the steak, well beaten with a cutlet bat, then the chopped onion, basil, parsley, bay leaf and mushrooms cut small; on this lay the tongue, and cover with the other half of the steak, well beaten, and over it pour the stock. Cover the saucepan and allow to cook very slowly for about three hours, adding more stock if necessary during that time, but allowing the broth to reduce almost to nothing by the end of the cooking period. Serve hot with a piquant sauce, or if preferred, lift on to a dish, allow to cool and serve cold with a green salad.

LINGUA CON OLIVE
Tongue with olives
TO SERVE 4

1 calf's tongue
1 carrot chopped
1 oz. butter
¼ pint boiling stock
1 small chopped onion
1 teaspoon chopped parsley
6 large green olives

Put the tongue in a stewpan, cover with cold water to which a little salt has been added; boil for 1½ hours, then drain, cool and skin. Melt the butter in a stewpan and in it brown the chopped vegetables; add the tongue and brown all over, then add the stock and the olives cut in small pieces, cover and allow to cook gently for a further 1½ hours, adding a little more stock from time to time if necessary.

Stuffed Meats

BRACIUOLE RIPIENE
Stuffed steak
TO SERVE 4

For the filling:
about 2 lbs. of veal steak cut in thin layers and flattened with a cutlet bat

about 2 ozs. of streaky bacon or lean ham
1 or 2 cloves of garlic, crushed
1 teaspoonful chopped parsley
2 ozs. grated Parmesan cheese
2 slices of bread, soaked in milk or water and squeezed dry
1 egg yolk
a pinch of nutmeg
pepper and salt

Chop the ham in small pieces, and to it add the other ingredients and mix well.

Cut the steak into strips about 7 inches in length and 3 inches in width, and on each spread a portion of the filling; roll the steak round the filling and fasten with thread or fine string.

In a heavy pan heat about 2 ozs. butter, and, if available, a little marrow from a bone, and in this place the rolls of steak, and allow to brown on all sides; add a chopped onion, a finely chopped carrot and a stalk of celery cut small; cover pan and allow to cook together for twenty minutes, adding, towards the end of the cooking time, a few tablespoons of good stock or strained tomato sauce.

VITELLO RIPIENO AL PASTICCIO
Stuffed veal pie
TO SERVE 4

For the stuffing:
about ¼ lb. lean veal
¼ lb. veal sweetbreads
¼ lb. lean ham
1 small onion chopped small
2 ozs. uncooked green peas
a pinch of marjoram
1 oz. butter
1 egg and three extra yolks
1 tablespoonful chopped parsley
¼ lb. mushrooms cut small

Heat the butter, and in it cook the onion until it is a golden colour; then add the veal, sweetbreads and ham, cut small, and cook together for ten or twelve minutes; remove from the stove and chop finely, then add the other ingredients.

Having prepared the above stuffing; take about 1½ lbs. of lean veal, cut in thin slices and pounded with a cutlet bat. Place a layer in a greased fireproof casserole, and on this place a layer of the stuffing, then a further layer of veal, and continue in this way till all is used up, finishing with a layer of veal; dot with butter, and bake in a moderate oven for three quarters of an hour, basting from time to time with a little good stock or strained tomato sauce. This may be eaten hot or cold.

Poultry & Game

Chicken

POLLO IN UMIDO
Chicken stew
TO SERVE 4

- 1 medium sized boiling fowl
- 1 stalk celery, cut small
- 1 teaspoon chopped parsley
- 1 tablespoon tomato conserve
- ¼ lb. mushrooms
- 1 small onion, chopped
- 1 carrot, chopped
- 1 oz. butter
- ½ pint stock or water
- pepper and salt

Clean and prepare the fowl and cut into joints for serving. Heat the butter in a stewpan and in it cook the chopped vegetables a few minutes; add the chicken and brown on all sides, then add the stock, the mushrooms cut small, and the tomato conserve diluted with a little stock or water. Cover the pan and simmer gently for 2 hours or until the chicken is tender, adding a little more stock if necessary during the cooking time.

POLLO ALLE OLIVE
Chicken with olives
TO SERVE 4

In addition to the ingredients for POLLO IN UMIDO in the preceding recipe, you will need six or eight large green olives. Proceed as in the preceding recipe but do not cut the fowl into joints, but leave it whole. After adding the stock, add the olives, stoned and cut in strips; allow the pan to simmer for 2 hours or until the chicken is tender, then serve on a heated dish with the sauce served in a separate tureen.

POLLO CON VERDURE
Garnished chicken
TO SERVE 4

- 1 medium sized boiling fowl
- 1 small onion, chopped small
- 1 level tablespoonful flour
- 1 tablespoon tomato conserve
- 2 stalks of celery
- ½ lb. pork sausages
- 2 slices streaky bacon
- 1 oz. butter
- ½ pint stock or water
- 1 carrot
- 1 small cabbage
- salt, pepper & nutmeg

Clean the fowl and cut in pieces for serving. Place the butter in a stewpan, heat it and in it cook the chopped onion till it is golden brown; add the pieces of chicken and allow to brown on all sides; stir in the flour and allow to cook a moment or two before adding the stock very slowly, stirring so as to prevent lumps forming; add the salt, pepper and nutmeg, the carrot and celery cut small; cover and cook slowly for 2 hours or until the chicken is tender; twenty minutes before serving, add the cabbage, washed and shredded, and the sausages, and when these are cooked, serve in a heated dish.

POLLO AI PISELLI
Chicken with peas

Prepare as for POLLO AI FUNGHI, but instead of the mushrooms add 1 pound of fresh green peas — weighed after shelling — and a tablespoonful of chopped parsley to the broth after the chicken is nearly cooked, and when the peas are cooked, serve the whole in a hot dish.

POLLO ALLA CREMA
Chicken with cream
TO SERVE 4

1 medium sized roasting fowl	flour
1 small onion	1 tablespoonful or more of butter
1 wineglassful of cream or 'top milk'	

Prepare the fowl, cut in pieces for serving. Heat the butter and in it brown the onion; then flour the pieces of chicken and brown on all sides in the heated butter, salting to taste. Add the cream and allow to cook to boiling point; remove from the stove and serve sprinkled with chopped parsley.

POLLO AI FUNGHI
Chicken with mushrooms
TO SERVE 4

1 medium sized boiling chicken	2 ozs. butter
1 small onion	½ pint stock or water
1 tablespoon tomato conserve	¼ lb. mushrooms

Prepare the chicken for cooking and cut in pieces. Heat the butter in a stewpan and in it cook the chopped onion until yellow. Lightly flour the chicken and fry in the butter until brown on all sides; salt to taste and add the stock and the tomato conserve diluted with a little stock. Cover and cook slowly for two hours or until the chicken is tender; lift the chicken from the gravy, and keep hot; meanwhile, clean the mushrooms and cut small, add them to the gravy and cook for ten minutes, then return the chicken to the stewpan, and when it has been in the gravy long enough for it to have come to the boil, serve in a hot dish.

PETTI DI POLLO ALLA LOMBARDA
Chicken breasts Lombardy style

TO SERVE 4

allow half a breast of chicken for each person
1 small onion
1 tablespoon chopped fennel
the livers of one or two chicken
1 oz. butter
1 teaspoon chopped parsley
1 lb. shelled green peas
½ pint hot stock or water
juice of ½ a lemon
2 egg yolks
pepper and salt

Heat the butter in a stewpan and in it brown the chopped onion and parsley; add the chicken, lightly floured, and brown on all sides, add the chopped fennel and the hot stock, cover and allow to cook for 25 minutes. Meanwhile cook the peas in boiling salted water for ten minutes, drain and add to the stewpan together with the chicken livers and seasoning; cook for a further ten minutes, then remove from the stove and stir in the beaten egg yolks mixed with the lemon juice. Serve immediately.

POLLO AL VINO BIANCO
Chicken with white wine

TO SERVE 4

Prepare a boiling fowl and cut in pieces, then lay on a flat dish and allow to marinate for at least 4 hours in a mixture of 1 wineglassful of white wine, a tablespoonful of olive oil, a pinch of nutmeg and salt to taste. Turn the chicken from time to time. At the end of 4 hours, place in a stewpan with a little butter and a cupful of stock, and cook slowly for at least 2 hours; finally thickening the broth with a little flour mixed with a little cold water, stirred into the stewpan and allowed to thicken, stirring all the time; finally add a little chopped parsley and serve hot.

CHICKEN AS SERVED IN ROME

TO SERVE 4

1 medium sized boiling fowl
4 tablespoons olive oil
1 sliced leek
a pinch of thyme
1 tablespoon tomato conserve
2 ozs. flour
4 cloves
a little chopped parsley
1 pint stock
4 ozs. macaroni
pepper and salt

Heat the oil in a large stewpan, and having prepared the chicken, add it to the stewpan with the chopped leek, cloves, herbs; allow it to brown on all sides, and take your time over this process. Pour off half the oil. Add the stock and the tomato conserve diluted with a little stock or water; cover and allow to finish cooking — at least another hour and a half or two hours, until the chicken is tender. Meanwhile cook and drain the macaroni, and when the chicken has finished cooking, remove it from the sauce and keep hot; add the macaroni to the sauce, mix well and serve around the chicken as a garnish.

PURÉE OF CHICKEN

For this, the breast of a medium sized chicken should be pounded in a mortar with a little stock, and two slices of bread that have been soaked in stock and squeezed dry. When well mixed, pass through a food mill, place in a stewpan with half a wineglassful of Marsala, and a similar amount of brown sauce and a pinch of mixed spice. Allow to cook gently for twenty minutes, remove from the heat and mix with a beaten egg yolk and the juice of half a lemon; season with salt and pepper to taste and serve on a dish surrounded by snippets of hot fried bread.

Game

HARE IN SWEET SOUR SAUCE

Skin and clean a hare, cut in pieces, wash in a weak solution of vinegar and water and flour lightly. Fry in butter in which you have browned a chopped onion and a slice of ham cut in small squares. Cover with stock and salt to taste and allow to cook slowly in a covered stewpan for about 1½ hours. Meanwhile mix together 2 tablespoons of sugar with half a wineglass full of vinegar, a heaped teaspoonful of grated bitter chocolate, a tablespoonful of chopped fennel and a few seedless raisins, mix well and add to the hare twenty minutes before serving.

HARE STEW

In a heavy stewpan heat an ounce of butter and in it brown a chopped onion and a crushed clove of garlic, a pinch of rosemary, a stalk of celery chopped fine, 2 tablespoons olive oil and a little chopped ham. Allow to cook together for several minutes, then add your hare cut in pieces, washed and lightly floured, and allow it to brown. Then slowly add a wineglassful of white wine, a little tomato conserve diluted with stock or water, half a pint of stock, half an ounce of dried mushrooms that have been soaked in water a few minutes, a pinch of nutmeg. Cover and allow to cook gently for 1½ to 2 hours.

PIGEONS WITH PEAS

Allow one pigeon per person, and when cleaned, brown them all over in a stewpan in hot butter to which has been added a chopped onion. Salt to taste and cover with boiling stock and a little tomato conserve diluted with stock or water. Cook gently for 1½ hours, then remove the pigeons and keep hot; meanwhile in the broth in which they have cooked, place half a pound of shelled green peas to every two pigeons, cook for twenty minutes, then replace the pigeons, allow to cook together a few minutes and serve hot. A little chopped basil is a welcome addition to this dish.

PERNICIOTTE ALLA MILANESE
Young partridges as cooked in Milan

Pluck and draw the birds and cut in two, lengthways, and flatten slightly with a cutlet bat. Allow them to marinate for an hour before cooking, in oil seasoned with salt, pepper, a little parsley and a crushed bay leaf. Then, one half at a time, dip in crisp breadcrumbs and fry on both sides in hot olive oil. Arrange on a heated dish and serve with anchovy sauce (See 'SAUCES').

BECCACCE AL SALMI
Woodcock

These tender little birds need plucking very carefully, and the head, which is left on the body, is skinned. They are NOT drawn before cooking.

Partly cook the woodcock in a stewpan with a little oil seasoned with salt, then cut in two, and remove the inside, throwing away the stomach and gall, but using the remainder to enrich the salmi, or sauce. Having removed the birds from the pan, heat a little butter, and in it brown a chopped onion and the insides removed from the birds and cut in small pieces; replace the birds, adding a very little stock to prevent the birds drying; cover and cook until tender. Serve garnished with snippets of toast spread with the salmi.

BECCACCE ALLA ROMAGNOLA
Another way with woodcock

For this recipe, having plucked the bodies and skinned the heads, remove the insides. Throw away the stomach and the gall, and put the remaining insides in a mortar with a little butter, four thin slices of ham cut in small pieces, a little chopped parsley and a little soft breadcrumb that has been soaked in water or milk and squeezed dry. Pound to a paste, season with pepper and salt and stuff the birds with the mixture, tying with thread or fine string, and twisting the head round so that the beak can be used as a skewer through the thighs. Wrap a piece of thin fat pork around the breast, sprinkle with salt, wrap in buttered paper and cook gently in a moderate oven for about an hour; remove the paper, dip the birds in beaten white of egg, sprinkle with crisp breadcrumbs and allow to cook for a further fifteen minutes so as to give them some colour.

Remove from the oven, remove the string or thread and serve accompanied with piquant sauce (See 'SAUCES'). and sections of lemon.

FAGIANO AL MADERA
Pheasant cooked in Madeira

Pluck and draw a pheasant, and place in a stewpan with four slices of fat bacon, and two slices of ham cut small, half an onion cut small, a stick of celery chopped fine, a teaspoonful of chopped parsley, a diced carrot and 1 ozs. butter, with pepper and salt and a dash of nutmeg. Cook together slowly until the pheasant begins to brown, then add a wineglassful of Madeira, and an equal quantity of stock; cover the stewpan and allow the bird to finish cooking — about three quarters of an hour. Then place the bird in a hot dish, strain the fat from the sauce, pass through a sieve and pour over the bird, and send to the table, garnished with croûtons of fried bread.

CONIGLIO ALLA BORGHESE
Rabbit 'Citizen' style

Skin a rabbit, removing the entrails. Cut the rabbit into joints, wash and wipe dry, and place in a stewpan with about an ounce of butter. Brown on all sides, then lower the heat and add a wineglassful of white wine, a chopped onion, a little chopped parsley, a pinch of thyme, a dash of nutmeg, pepper and salt, and either quarter of a pound of fresh mushrooms cut small, or half an ounce of dried mushrooms 'revived' in a little broth and cut small. Cover the stewpan, and allow to cook slowly for $1\frac{1}{2}$ hours, adding a little stock from time to time if it looks as through the rabbit is drying out.

CONIGLIO IN SALSA PICCANTE
Rabbit in piquant sauce

Cut the rabbit into joints, flour these, and place in a stewpan in which 2 ounces of butter have been heated. Allow the rabbit to brown on all sides, then add a stick of celery, chopped fine, a little chopped parsley, a small onion, a carrot cut small, $\frac{1}{4}$ lb. mushrooms cut small, two or three cloves, pepper, salt and a pinch of nutmeg. Add a wineglassful of red wine and an equal quantity of stock; cover the stewpan and allow to cook for about an hour, then remove the pieces of rabbit; pass the gravy through a sieve, pressing it through with a wooden spoon so as not to leave behind anything but the 'dregs', add a couple of tablespoons of capers and two anchovies that have been pounded in a mortar; mix well, replace in the stewpan with the pieces of rabbit, and allow to boil for a few minutes more. Serve surrounded by croûtons of toast or fried bread.

FRICASSÉE OF RABBIT

Heat an ounce of butter in a stewpan, and in it fry a tablespoonful of butter until brown, then add a rabbit, cut into joints and floured, together with a couple of slices of fat bacon cut small, and allow to cook until the rabbit has browned — say 15 minutes. Cover with a wineglassful of white wine and an equal quantity of stock, add a chopped onion and a pinch of pepper, and cook fairly slowly until the liquid is reduced by half and the rabbit is tender. Remove the rabbit on to a hot dish, remove the pan from the fire and into the sauce mix the beaten yolks of two eggs and the juice of half a lemon. Mix well and pour over the rabbit before serving.

CONIGLIO IN SALSA PICCANTE
Rabbit in piquant sauce

Prepare the rabbit by skinning, cleaning, cutting into pieces, washing and wiping dry with a cloth. Place in a stewpan with 4 ounces of butter, after having floured it lightly; allow to brown for about quarter of an hour, then add a couple of sticks of celery cut in thin slices, a heaped teaspoonful of chopped fresh parsley, a medium sized onion chopped finely, a medium sized carrot cut in thin slices, quarter of a pound of fresh mushrooms, three cloves, salt to taste and a pinch of nutmeg. Add a wineglassful of red wine and an equal quantity of hot stock, cover the stewpan and allow to cook for an hour or until the rabbit is tender. Remove the rabbit and keep warm; pour the broth through a food mill into another stewpan, add to it two anchovies cut in pieces and two tablespoons of capers, heat together for a few minutes, return the rabbit to the broth and allow to cook together for a few minutes longer; serve on a heated dish surrounded by snippets of toast.

Vegetables

Where vegetables are concerned, the Italian cook is considerably more imaginative than her English counterpart, and one is unlikely to be confronted with 'plain boiled' potatoes, or with watery vegetable marrow served with a thin white sauce; try some of these suggestions for livening up the vegetable dishes.

CARCIOFI
Artichokes

Globe artichokes, a luxury in England, are one of Italy's staple vegetables. In Sicily one can pass acres and acres of land planted with these delicious vegetables; small wonder that they make frequent appearances on the Italian menu.

To prepare them for cooking, remove the outer leaves, cut off half of the top, or point of the artichoke, cut in halves and then in quarters, and allow to remain for about half an hour in water to which you have added a little lemon juice or vinegar. Drain and place in a saucepan with a little oil, a little lemon juice, salt, pepper, a clove of garlic, crushed, and a pinch of origano, allow the artichokes to cook for fifteen minutes, turning them frequently so that they become golden brown all over; remove to a hot dish and keep warm and to the sauce add one or two anchovies cut in small pieces, and cook together for a few minutes, then pour over the artichokes and serve hot.

CARCIOFI IN FRICASSEA
Fricassée of artichokes

Prepare the artichokes by removing the outer leaves, and cutting off half or a little more of the pointed end; leave for half an hour in water to which you have added a little lemon juice. Drain, and place in a saucepan with a little butter, chopped parsley, a clove of garlic crushed, and salt to taste. Allow to cook slowly for three quarters of an hour, then remove the pan from the heat, and add one or two egg yolks (depending on the quantity of artichokes) beaten lightly with a teaspoon of water per egg yolk, the juice of half a lemon, and a tablespoonful of grated Parmesan cheese. Serve very hot.

CARCIOFI IN UMIDO CON PISELLI
Artichokes stewed with peas
TO SERVE 4

12 globe artichokes
¾ lb. shelled fresh peas, weighed after shelling
3 egg yolks
1 tablespoon olive oil
1 small onion
chopped parsley
juice of half a lemon
¼ pint stock or water

Prepare the artichokes; meanwhile, chop the onion and fry lightly in the oil, together with the parsley; add the artichokes, quartered, the peas and the stock together with pepper and salt. Cook together for half an hour, stirring from time to time so that the vegetables do not stick to the bottom of the pan; at the end of the cooking time, remove from the heat and stir in the beaten yolks of eggs and the lemon juice and serve hot.

CARCIOFI ALLA GIUDAICA
Jewish Artichokes
TO SERVE 4

Prepare a dozen artichokes, leaving a fairly long stem. While they are soaking, prepare a 'battuto' with a little chopped parsley, a little chopped mint, a crushed clove of garlic, and place a little of this in the middle of each artichoke after draining the vegetable. In a deep pan heat a cupful of olive oil very hot and in this place the artichokes upside down, pressing them down so that the leaves spread out. Cook over a hot flame for ten minutes and serve with sections of lemon.

ASPARAGI ALL'OLIO
Asparagus with oil

Remove the hard end of the stalks of a bundle of asparagus, and remove the 'scales' that are to be found along the stalks; tie in smaller bundles with fine string and boil gently in salted water for about twenty minutes. Remove from the water, cut the string and remove and serve with either melted butter or olive oil.

ASPARAGI ALLA MILANESE
Asparagus Milanese Style

Having prepared and cooked your bundle of asparagus, drain, and lay in a fireproof dish, with a lump of butter, pepper and salt and place in a hot oven for a few moments; just before serving, sprinkle with two tablespoons of grated Parmesan cheese, and serve as soon as this starts to melt.

FAGIOLINI AL BURRO
Buttered French Beans
TO SERVE 4

1 lb. young French beans
2 ozs. butter
2 tablespoons grated Parmesan
pepper and salt

Top and tail the beans, and cook them in boiling salted water for twenty minutes; drain, and place in a greased fireproof dish with the butter, pepper and salt and grated cheese, and place in a moderate oven until the cheese starts to melt. Serve immediately.

FAGIOLINI IN FRICASSEA
Fricassée of French Beans
TO SERVE 4

1 lb. French beans
1 tablespoonful chopped parsley
1 clove garlic, crushed
juice of half a lemon
1 tablespoonful grated Parmesan

2 ozs. butter
salt and pepper
1 or 2 egg yolks, beaten lightly with a teaspoon of cold water per yolk

Prepare the beans and cook in boiling salted water for fifteen minutes, then drain, and place in a stewpan with the parsley, butter, garlic and salt; allow to cook gently for a further ten minutes, remove from the heat and stir in the beaten egg yolks, lemon juice and grated cheese and serve immediately.

FAGIOLINI ALLA ROMANA
French beans, Roman style
TO SERVE 4

1 lb. young French beans
1 medium onion chopped small

1 oz. butter
pepper, salt and nutmeg
2 anchovies cut small

Prepare the beans and boil in salted water for fifteen minutes, saving a little of the cooking water, and drain. Place in a stewpan in which you have prepared a 'battuto' of the butter, onion, seasonings and chopped anchovies, together with a little of the water in which the beans were cooked; cook gently for ten minutes, during which time the liquid will have reduced in quantity, remove from the fire and serve.

FAGIOLI ALLA PROVINCIALE
Haricot beans
TO SERVE 4

1 pint of haricot beans, which have been allowed to soak overnight in cold water

1 small onion chopped small
1 teaspoonful chopped parsley
2 ozs. butter
1 clove garlic, crushed

Drain the beans and cook in boiling, salted water for about an hour or until tender; drain. Meanwhile, in a stewpan heat the butter and in it brown the chopped onion and garlic, add the drained beans and the parsley, add pepper and salt to taste and the tomato sauce. Cook together for a further ten minutes.

HARICOT BEANS WITH BACON
TO SERVE 4

12 ozs. haricot beans, soaked overnight, and cooked till tender in boiling salted water, using a pint of water, and cooking for about an hour — do not throw away the water in which they have been cooked but place in a fireproof casserole and add:
1 teaspoon dry mustard

3 tablespoonsful molasses or black treacle
3 ozs. brown sugar
salt to taste
2 tablespoonsfuls vinegar
2 tablespoonsful tomato conserve moistened with 4 tablespoonsful warm water
4 ozs. bacon or ham cut in small squares
1 small onion chopped fine

Cover and cook in a really slow oven (Regulo 1 is quite hot enough) for six or eight hours, looking at them from time to time and adding more water if they appear to be becoming too dry.

FAVE AL GUNCIALE
Broad Beans with bacon
TO SERVE 4

2 lbs. broad beans, and if you wish really to enjoy them, gather them while they are still small and tender

2 slices of streaky bacon
1 oz. butter
1 medium sized onion

Heat the butter in a stewpan, in it cook the chopped onion until it is a golden yellow colour, add the bacon cut in dice, and when this is cooked, add the shelled uncooked beans, and cook together for a further five minutes; add water almost to cover; place lid on stewpan and simmer gently for twenty minutes. Add pepper and salt to taste.

PISELLI AL PROSCIUTTO
Green Peas with Ham
TO SERVE 4

2 lbs. peas
1 small onion

$\frac{1}{4}$ lb. ham cut in dice
1 oz. butter

Melt the butter in a stewpan, cook the chopped onion till a golden yellow; add the diced ham and cook for a further five minutes, then add the peas, shelled, washed but not cooked; add sufficient water not quite to cover, and cook gently for quarter of an hour with the lid on the stewpan.

PISELLI ALLA PARIGINA
Peas, Paris style
TO SERVE 4

A French recipe, but one which finds its way into Italian cookery books and on to Italian tables, so well worth including.

2 lbs. peas
4 spring onions
salt and pepper

2 round lettuce
2 teaspoons castor sugar
1 oz. butter

Shell the peas, and retain four or five of the best-looking shells. Wash the lettuce and cut in four lengthways, then lift it out of the water and place it dripping wet in a stewpan in which you have already warmed the butter, add the peas and the pea pods you have kept aside, the onions and pepper and salt; cover and allow to cook slowly for forty-five minutes, shaking the pan from time to time to prevent the vegetables sticking. Take a look from time to time, and if the peas look like becoming dry, add a teaspoonful or two of warm water. Five minutes before serving, add the sugar and shake the pan to mix well.

Aubergines

These luscious-looking vegetables make delicious eating cooked in various ways.

MELANZANE ALLA GENOVESE
Aubergine Genoese style
TO SERVE 4

3 or 4 medium sized aubergines
1 chopped onion
pepper and salt

1 tablespoon olive oil
2 or 3 ripe tomatoes

Heat the oil and in it cook the chopped onion until it is golden brown; add the aubergines, cut in half-inch slices crossways and cook for five minutes, then add the tomatoes, peeled and cut in pieces, and cook together until the egg plant is tender; remove from the fire and stir in two lightly beaten eggs; mix well and serve immediately.

MELANZANE ALLA NAPOLITANA
Aubergine, Neapolitan style
TO SERVE 4

> 3 or 4 medium sized aubergines
> ¼ lb. Bel Paese, unless you are in Italy, in which case use an equal quantity of Mozzarella
> pepper and salt
> 2 ozs. grated Parmesan
> ¾ pint or rather more tomato sauce

For this dish peel the aubergines, cut in half-inch slices crossways, sprinkle with salt, cover and leave for an hour or so, then drain, flour lightly and fry gently in hot olive oil, then drain on blotting paper to remove the surplus oil.

Grease or oil a soufflé dish or fireproof casserole and in it put alternate layers of aubergines, Bel Paese cheese and tomato sauce until all is used up; sprinkle with the grated Parmesan and dot with butter. Bake in a moderate oven for twenty-five minutes.

MELANZANE RIPIENE
Stuffed aubergine
TO SERVE 4

> 2 large aubergines
> 1 small onion chopped
> 2 slices of ham diced
> 1 oz. butter
> 2 slices of bread, soaked in milk and squeezed dry
> ¼ lb. chopped mushrooms
> pepper and salt

Split the aubergines in two lengthways and scoop out the middle of the flesh, and place on one side. Meanwhile, heat the butter in a small pan. In it cook the chopped onion until it is a golden yellow, add the tomatoes, cut small, the chopped mushrooms and the ham, and sauté together for five minutes. Add the bread and the flesh of the aubergines cut small and mix well together, adding pepper and salt to taste. Fill the aubergines with the mixture, lay in a fireproof baking dish side by side, dot with butter and bake in a slow oven for about an hour.

CIPOLLE RIPIENE
Stuffed onions
TO SERVE 4

For this you need the large Spanish type onion, allowing one per person. Cook them in boiling water for 15 minutes, drain, remove the centre and fill with stuffing as suggested for aubergines, adding a few chopped black olives if liked. Place in a fireproof baking dish, dot with butter and bake in a slow oven for an hour.

POTATO PANCAKES
TO SERVE 4

4 large potatoes
2 tablespoons flour

2 medium sized onions
pepper and salt to taste

Grate the raw potatoes, draining off any surplus liquid; add the chopped or grated onion, flour and seasoning, mixing thoroughly. Drop by spoonfuls into very hot oil in a frying pan and cook golden brown.

PATATE IN STUFATO
Sautéed potatoes
TO SERVE 4

4 large potatoes
2 tablespoons butter
1 tablespoonful tomato conserve
a slice of fat roast beef
a teaspoonful of chopped rosemary

Heat the butter in a stewpan, add the beef cut in dice and fry till brown. Then add the potatoes peeled and cut in thin slices, and the rosemary, pepper and salt, and finally the tomato conserve thinned with a little water; cook over moderate heat for three-quarters of an hour, stirring now and again and adding a little boiling water if the dish appears to be drying.

POTATO FRITTERS

1 lb. potatoes
2 whole eggs and 2 extra yolks
2 ozs. butter
a few chopped pistachio or pine nuts

Cook the potatoes and mash in a pestle and mortar or pass through a ricer, adding the butter, beaten eggs and chopped nuts. Form into small rissoles, dip in egg-white and fry in hot olive oil. Drain and serve very hot.

PATATE ARROSTO
Baked potatoes
TO SERVE 4

Allow one good-sized potato per person; peel and place in a baking dish with an ounce or more of butter, and bake in a moderate oven for an hour or until they are nicely browned but not burnt; baste from time to time with the butter and sprinkle lightly with salt.

PATATE CON SALSA DI POMIDORO
Potatoes with tomato sauce
TO SERVE 4

4 large potatoes
1 medium sized onion, chopped

½ pint tomato sauce
1 tablespoon oil

Heat the oil and in it cook the chopped onion till a golden brown; add the potatoes, peeled and cut in slices, simmer for a few minutes, then add the tomato sauce, together with a little water and cook gently till the potatoes are tender and the liquid has reduced and thickened — about 40 minutes.

PATATE AL BURRO
Buttered potatoes
TO SERVE 4

4 large potatoes
1 tablespoon chopped parsley

3 tablespoons stock
2 ozs. butter

Peel the potatoes and cut in slices, and place in a stewpan with the stock and the parsley and cook over moderate heat until the potatoes are cooked, adding a little water from time to time if they appear to be drying up; five minutes before serving add the butter. Mix well together and serve hot.

TOMATOES COOKED WITH ONIONS
TO SERVE 4

1 large tin tomatoes
salt and pepper
1 tablespoon castor sugar

1 oz. butter
3 medium sized onions
1 cupful breadcrumbs

Drain the tomatoes, saving the liquid to add to the stock pot. Sprinkle the tomatoes with salt, pepper and sugar. Peel and slice the onions, and in a buttered fireproof dish arrange alternate layers of tomatoes, onions and breadcrumbs, finishing with a layer of breadcrumbs. Dot with butter and bake in a moderate oven for half an hour.

POMIDORI ALLA CASALINGA
Tomatoes, housewife style
TO SERVE 4

- 1 lb. firm tomatoes
- a pinch of oregano
- salt and pepper
- 1 tablespoon olive oil
- 1 clove garlic, crushed
- 1 tablespoon chopped parsley
- 1 tablespoon grated Parmesan

Halve the tomatoes, removing the seeds; place in a greased fireproof dish, sprinkling with a mixture of salt, pepper, oregano, garlic and parsley, and finally with the grated cheese and oil; bake in moderate oven twenty minutes.

CAROTE AL BURRO
Buttered carrots
TO SERVE 4

- 1 lb. young carrots, washed and scraped and cut in slices
- 1 oz. butter
- 3 tablespoons stock
- a pinch of cinnamon
- salt and pepper
- 1 tablespoonful flour
- juice of half a lemon

Boil the carrots in salted water for quarter of an hour, drain, and place in a buttered fireproof dish with the butter, pepper and salt, stir in the flour and gently add the stock, and allow to cook in a moderate oven or on top of the stove for ten minutes; finally, five minutes before serving, add the cinnamon and lemon juice.

CARROTS COOKED IN BUTTER

For this you need carrots that are not too tiny. Peel the carrots and cut in lengthways strips, cook for ten minutes in boiling, salted water, then drain, and place in a stewpan with a good knob of butter, pepper and salt. Allow them to cook gently in the butter for ten minutes, then add two or three tablespoonfuls of meat stock that has been thickened with a little flour. At the end of another ten minutes, during which you have stirred the pan to prevent the carrots sticking, add a little cayenne pepper and sprinkle with the juice of half a lemon before serving.

CANDIED CARROTS

Peel carrots and cut in dice; cook in boiling, salted water for ten minutes; drain. Heat a little butter in a heavy pan, add the carrots, and over them sprinkle a little brown sugar. Cook slowly, stirring from time to time to prevent sticking, until the carrots are glazed and tender. A little Marsala is a welcome addition, but if this is used, allow to evaporate, so that in the finished dish you have the carrots glazed, tender, but not liquid.

BRUSSELS SPROUTS SERVED WITH CHESTNUTS
TO SERVE 4

2 lbs. good, hard Brussels sprouts	½ lb. chestnuts
1 tablespoon brown sugar	3 ozs. butter
	1 tablespoon flour
	salt

Cook the sprouts in boiling salted water, and when draining them save about half a pint of the water in which they have been cooked. Meanwhile, blanch and peel the chestnuts and boil in salted water until tender — about twenty-five minutes. Heat the butter in a small stewpan and in it brown the flour; stir in the sugar and mix well, then slowly add the half pint of water from the sprouts, and stir until the mixture thickens. Mix the chestnuts and sprouts together, cover with this sauce, and place in a warm oven until heated through.

BROCCOLI STRASCICATI
Broccoli with salt pork

Prepare the broccoli and cook in boiling salted water for fifteen minutes; drain. Place in a stewpan with a little salt pork cut in dice and cook over a very slow fire for half an hour until the fat has been absorbed by the broccoli. No further salting will be necessary, as there will be sufficient salt in the pork.

CAVOLFIORE ALLA SICILIANA
Cauliflower Sicilian style

Cook your cauliflower for fifteen minutes in boiling, slightly salted water, drain, and place in a greased fireproof dish two anchovies chopped small, place in moderate oven and bake for fifteen minutes, basting with a little oil from time to time; finally add three tablespoons of tomato sauce and a few capers and allow to cook a few minutes longer before serving. Send to the table in the dish in which it has been cooked.

CAVOLFIORE ALLA LIONESE
Cauliflower with meat sauce
TO SERVE 4

1 good-sized cauliflower

½ pint meat sauce (See 'SAUCES')

Cook the cauliflower for ten minutes only in boiling salted water, then drain and place in cold water for a few minutes; drain again and break into small pieces, and place in a stewpan with the meat sauce and allow to cook a further twenty minutes over moderate heat, adding a little stock or water if it appears to be getting too dry.

PUREE OF CHESTNUTS
TO SERVE 6

1 lb. of chestnuts from which outer and inner skins have been removed
a little warm milk
salt and pepper
1 oz. butter

Boil the chestnuts in salted water until tender, then drain, and mash with just enough warm milk to moisten them; add butter and pepper and salt to taste. Serve instead of mashed potatoes.

MARROWS

Whenever I am faced with a helping of boiled marrow, served in the English fashion, with white sauce, I think fondly of the more enterprising Italian ways of dealing with this vegetable. To our credit be it said that from the colossal ripe marrows of the late season we English can produce marrow pickle and marrow preserve that would bear comparison with any similar Continental delicacies, but what we do with early marrow is, to say the least, a trifle uninteresting.

In the fruit and vegetables shops during the summer the tiny imported 'zucchini' are to be seen, and may be bought at luxury prices, but there is no reason why our English marrows should not be harvested while they are still young and tender and used in recipes for which 'zucchini' have been prescribed. Take for example some of the following:

ZUCCHINE FRITTI
Fried small marrows
TO SERVE 4

You need either a pound of zucchine, or a small English marrow of equal weight. Cut into rounds about $\frac{3}{8}$ths of an inch thick, spread on a plate, and cover with a sprinkling of salt. Place an inverted plate over them and leave for an hour, by the end of which time the liquid will have come out of them. Drain thoroughly, then flour them and fry them in hot olive oil, allowing about a minute for each side. Drain them well before serving, so as to remove surplus oil, and serve with sections of lemon.

STUFFED MARROW
TO SERVE 4

1 lb. small marrows
chopped ham
breadcrumbs

pepper and salt and a pinch of rosemary mixed well together

Split the marrows in two lengthways, and remove the seeds. Fill the hollows with the stuffing, put the two halves of the marrows together again and tie with white cotton to keep the stuffing in. Heat a little butter in a stewpan, add the marrows, brown them lightly, then reduce the heat and cover the pan, and cook for a further twenty minutes.

STEWED SMALL MARROWS
TO SERVE 4

1 lb. small marrows
3 tablespoons olive oil

3 good-sized onions
¼ pint water
pepper and salt to taste

Heat the oil and in it cook the chopped onion until it is golden brown. Add the marrows, unpeeled if you have the actual zucchine or supposing you are using English marrows these too may be unpeeled provided they are quite small, but if you are using the larger variety, then peel and cut into 1-inch slices; add water and seasoning; cover the pan and cook slowly for half an hour.

MARROW WITH TOMATO

As a variation of the above dish, omit the water and add instead of it either two large tomatoes peeled and sliced, or a small tin of tomatoes, and if procurable, a teaspoonful of chopped basil, or failing this, a similar amount of chopped parsley. Keep an eye on the dish while cooking, and if it looks as though it is drying out, add a very little water from time to time.

SPINACH

Remember the need of washing spinach thoroughly; seven waters was at one time prescribed, and unless the spinach is phenomenally free from grit and sand, seven waters will not prove to be too many. To cook so as to retain as much as possible of the natural flavour, do not place the spinach in water, but after the last washing, lift it from the vessel with the hands, shake it well and place it in a saucepan large enough to hold the mass, without the addition of further water; sprinkle salt and cook over a low heat for ten or fifteen minutes, pressing it down from time to time with a fork to ensure even cooking.

SPINACH AS SERVED IN ROME
TO SERVE 4

Having cooked a pound of spinach as directed for ten minutes, add to it three tablespoons of good olive oil, and pepper and salt to taste. Mix well and serve very hot.

SPINACI ALLA PARMIGIANA
Spinach with Parmesan cheese
TO SERVE 4

1 lb. spinach
salt, pepper and
 nutmeg

butter
2 tablespoons grated
 Parmesan

Cook the spinach as directed, and when cooked drain well, then place in a stewpan with about two ounces of butter, salt, pepper and a pinch of nutmeg. Allow the butter to melt, then stir in the grated cheese and serve hot.

SPINACI ALLA PIEMONTESE
TO SERVE 4

1 lb. spinach
1 oz. butter or
 1 tablespoonful
 olive oil
salt and pepper to
 taste

6 or 8 anchovies
 cut small
half a clove of
 garlic, crushed

Cook the spinach as directed and drain well. Heat the butter in a pan, add the garlic and cook till yellow, add the spinach, anchovies and pepper and salt to taste, mix well together, and serve decorated with triangles of thin toast.

Salads

The salad most commonly met with in Italy is the fresh green salad, liberally doused with good olive oil and lemon juice, but there are a fair number of other salads to be met with when one spends a longer time in the country, and here are a few suggestions.

ONION SALAD

Allow one large or two medium sized onions per person.
 Either bake the onions in the oven, or boil them until they are cooked but not mushy. Allow to cool and when cold, slice them fairly thinly, spread in layers on a flat dish and season with olive oil, lemon juice and pepper and salt.

PLAIN SALAD

Cos or Batavian lettuce, washed well and hung in a salad drainer until crisp, is excellent by itself served with a plain oil and vinegar dressing, mixed well. (See 'DRESSING FOR GREEN SALAD'.)

SALAD WITH HARD BOILED EGG

Allow one hard boiled egg per person, cut in two lengthways and arrange on top of a bed of lettuce dressed as previously suggested with an oil and vinegar dressing; or if liked, serve individual plates of dressed lettuce, with egg, cut lengthways decorating each portion.
With all green salads, remember not to add the dressing until the last possible moment before serving, and remember, too, that torn lettuce is preferable to lettuce cut with knife or scissors.

CUCUMBER SALAD

Slice thinly an unpeeled cucumber; spread the slices in a flat plate, sprinkle with salt, cover with another plate and leave for about two hours. Drain, and squeeze moisture out of the slices by placing in a cloth and squeezing in the hands. Season with oil, wine vinegar (or lemon juice), pepper and salt to taste, and, for additional enjoyment, a little castor sugar.

MIXED SALAD

Slice thinly a few gherkins, and a green pepper, add some cooked meat — ham, veal, pork or chicken for preference — cut in small pieces, a few cold boiled new potatoes, and if liked one or two anchovies, boned and cut small. Mix well together and serve with an oil and vinegar dressing.

MIXED SALAD WITH HARD BOILED EGG

Take three or four cold boiled potatoes (not floury ones), a beetroot cooked in the oven and cooled. Cut the vegetables into dice, and to them add two small gherkins, cut in thin slices. Combine these with a head of endive, washed carefully and torn into pieces. Mix well, and toss in an oil and vinegar dressing; sprinkle with capers, and decorate with three or four anchovies, and one hard boiled egg per person, peeled and cut in two lengthways.

INSALATA ALLA GIARDINIERA
Gardener's wife's salad

Mix together any left-over cooked young vegetables, small young potatoes, peas, beans, etc. together with peeled, sliced tomatoes, and serve with a dressing of oil and vinegar, pepper and salt.

SALAD WITH SOUR CREAM

When eggs are plentiful, hard-boil half a dozen, and having passed the yolks through a sieve, mix with half a cup or thereabouts of sour cream; add a pinch of salt, freshly-ground black pepper and two teaspoons or a little more of wine vinegar, and use as a salad dressing on a mixture of lettuce and sliced fresh cucumber.

Sweets

Sweets met with on vacation in Italy seem to be of two kinds; either the welcome, well-filled dish of fruits in season, or the out-size very rich, very creamy 'layer cake', but a longer stay discloses other, more imaginative sweets, and a selection of these is given in the following pages.

ZABAGLIONE or ZABAIONE

When talking of sweets in the Italian menu, this airy-fairy refinement of egg punch is the one that springs first to the mind, and it is worth while knowing how to make it to perfection.

For each consumer allow 2 egg yolks, 2 tablespoons castor sugar, and 2 tablespoons of Marsala, or failing this, of good Sherry. Vanilla may be added, if liked, but for my taste the dish is better without it.

Beat together the egg yolks and sugar until they are pale and creamy, then slowly add the Marsala. Place the mixture over hot water in a double boiler, and stir slowly until it thickens, taking care not to overcook it, otherwise it will curdle. Serve immediately in warmed sherbet glasses. There is a school of thought that dictates 'serve hot or cold', but this to most Italian palates is heresy — serve your zabaione hot.

Fritters

Starting off with a frying batter as a basis, delicious fritters may be made of the various fruits as they come into season.

STANDARD FRYING BATTER

4 ozs. plain flour
a quarter of a pint or rather more of warm water

3 tablespoons olive oil
a pinch of salt
1 lightly beaten egg white

Sieve the flour into a basin, make a well in the centre and into this pour the oil; mix well, and add the salt, then slowly add the water, stirring constantly until the consistency of thick cream is obtained. Allow to stand for 2 hours or thereabouts, then stir in the lightly beaten egg white, and use as a coating for fish or for fruits as suggested in the following pages.

APPLE FRITTERS

For these use Bramleys or similar large cooking apples, allowing one per person. Peel the apples, and remove the core with a metal corer, then slice the apples transversely in slices about three-eighths of an inch in thickness, dip in batter, and fry in hot oil; drain, sprinkle with castor sugar and serve very hot.

An improvement is to substitute for half the water of the batter, an equal amount of white wine.

A refinement of these fritters also is to be obtained by immersing the apples, once they are peeled and cored, but before slicing them, in rum to which sugar and a pinch of cinnamon has been added, allowing them to remain for two or three hours, turning them frequently so as to impregnate the fruit with the rum, but in this case, the water batter is sufficiently rich without the addition of white wine.

PEAR FRITTERS

Using the same method, but instead of slicing the fruit, peel them, quarter them and core them before dipping in batter, hard cooking pears make delicious fritters.

APRICOT FRITTERS

For these the apricots should not be over-ripe. Cut in two, removing the stones; place in a vessel deep enough to hold them when sprinkled with sugar; leave for several hours, or even for a whole day, then remove and drain, dip in frying batter and fry in hot oil, drain and serve, hot sprinkled with castor sugar.

Alternatively, instead of covering with sugar and leaving for some hours, the apricots may be covered with rum, to which has been added sugar and a pinch of cinnamon, left for two or three hours, then drained, dipped in batter and fried.

PEACH FRITTERS

Peel the peaches, halve them and remove the stone. Immerse for several hours in white wine to which sugar has been added; remove, drain, dip in frying batter and fry in hot olive oil.

FIG FRITTERS

For these you need fresh figs that are not overripe. Cut the fruit in two lengthways, and spread on a plate, sprinkling them with sugar and with a few drops of a good liqueur, Benedictine, Rosolio, or some similar liqueur. Leave for two or three hours, then drain, sprinkle lightly with flour, dip in frying batter, and fry in hot oil; drain and serve hot, sprinkled with castor sugar.

PLUM FRITTERS

Again use fruit that is not over-ripe. Place in a warm oven for half an hour, then cut in halves, remove the stones, and spread on a dish, sprinkling with sugar and a few drops of rum and a pinch of cinnamon. Leave for two or three hours, then drain, dip in frying batter and fry as directed for the previous fruit fritters.

SEMOLINA FRITTERS

1 pint milk
pinch salt
4 egg yolks
a little candied citron
4 tablespoons sugar
4 ozs. semolina
2 egg whites
2 ozs. raisins

Heat the milk with the sugar and salt and when it begins to boil, place in the top of a double boiler, and add the semolina little by little until a thick paste is formed, stirring continually so that it does not stick to the bottom of the saucepan; remove from the heat, cool slightly and add the beaten egg yolks and later the whites beaten stiffly, the citron cut small and the raisins. Mix together well, and when cool, form into little balls the size of a walnut; dip in beaten egg white and then in breadcrumbs and fry quickly in deep oil until a golden brown; drain for a moment or two on blotting paper to drain off any surplus oil, and serve hot, sprinkled liberally with castor sugar.

CHESTNUT FRITTERS

To half a pound of chestnut flour, add sufficient water to make a thick paste; add a pinch of salt, a few seedless raisins, and a few chopped pistachio nuts; mix together well and drop in spoonfuls into deep hot oil, cooking till golden brown. Drain and serve hot, sprinkled with castor sugar.

FRITTELLE ALLA FIORENTINA

To half a pound of fine flour add sufficient water to make a thick paste; add a pinch of salt, the yolk of an egg, a little grated lemon rind and a few seedless raisins. Mix well and drop in spoonfuls into deep hot oil and fry until golden brown; Drain and serve hot.

SWEET FRITTERS

2 egg yolks
1 pint cream
2 tablespoons sugar

2 ozs. flour
a little finely chopped candied citron

Beat together the egg yolks, cream and sugar until well mixed, blend in the flour and place in a double boiler, cooking till thick and being careful not to allow it to boil, otherwise the egg yolks will curdle. If the cream does not seem to be thick enough, a little semolina may be added towards the end of the cooking time. Stir in the citron.

Pour on to a flat plate that has been lightly oiled or greased with butter; allow to cool, cut in pieces about two inches square; dip in white of egg and then in breadcrumbs, fry in butter till golden brown, serve hot, sprinkled with sugar.

MONT BLANC
THIS SHOULD SERVE 4

1 lb. Italian chestnuts
¼ pint double cream

½ lb. castor sugar

Cut a slit in the chestnuts at the pointed end, and place them a dozen at a time in a very hot oven for ten minutes, after which they will peel easily. When all are peeled, place in boiling water and allow to simmer for an hour or until they are tender. Strain, and mash the nuts, adding the sugar and a pinch of salt. Pass them then through a potato ricer, allowing them to pile up in pyramid form on a dish. The less you touch them with your hands the better, otherwise the light appearance of the finished dish is apt to be spoiled.

Whip the cream, flavouring it if you like with a little good liqueur, and pile it lightly on the top of the mound of chestnuts, rather like snow on a mountain top.

CHARLOTTE DI MELE, PERE O PESCHE

Apple, pear or peach charlotte

TO SERVE 6

- 2 lbs. cooking apples, pears or peaches that are not over-ripe
- grated rind of a lemon
- 1 wineglassful rum
- 4 ozs. brown sugar
- 1 tablespoon cold water
- 1 oz. butter
- 1 wineglassful white wine
- thin slices of bread and butter with crusts removed

Prepare the fruit by peeling and coring (or in the case of peaches, removing the stones), put them in a stewpan with the sugar, the water and the white rind and cook until tender; when the fruit is reduced to a pulp, add the butter and the grated lemon rind, and if not sufficiently sweet add a little more sugar. Meanwhile, grease a soufflé mould, and line it entirely with well-buttered slices of thin bread. Pour in the fruit pulp, and over the top place a layer of thinly sliced and buttered bread. Sprinkle with sugar. Bake in a moderate oven for half an hour, and just before serving, pour over the rum and light, so that the dish is carried flaming to the table. This final touch may be omitted if preferred.

BODINO DI LATTE ALLA MANDORLE
Milk pudding with almonds
TO SERVE 4

For those who like almonds, here is a refinement of milk pudding that is worthy of attention.

- 1 pint milk
- 2 ozs. almonds
- 2 slices of bread with crust removed, soaked in milk and squeezed dry
- butter for greasing a soufflé dish
- 4 to 5 ozs. castor sugar, depending on personal taste
- 6 whole eggs and two extra yolks
- a little candied citron

Blanch the almonds in boiling water and remove the skins, then in a mortar pound them to a paste, uniting them with the soaked and squeezed bread. Meanwhile heat the milk in a double boiler, with the sugar added; when the milk reaches boiling point, add the paste of almonds and bread, little by little, and cook a few minutes longer, stirring so that it does not stick to the bottom of the pan. Remove from the fire and slowly add the beaten eggs and extra yolks, mixing well. Meanwhile, grease your soufflé dish, and pour in the milk mixture, and cook for an hour in an oven that is not too fierce (the heat you use for rice pudding should be right for this).
Serve hot, and if you wish to make it even more luxurious, prepare a zabaglione, and serve at the same time.

BODINO DI GABINETTO
Cabinet pudding
TO SERVE 4

Sufficient stale Savoy fingers to line your soufflé mould, which should be the pint-and-a-half size

¼ lb. ratafia biscuits
2 whole eggs and
  2 extra yolks
grated rind of half
  a lemon
a few glacé cherries
  and a little shred-
  ded angelica

¾ pint milk
1 tablespoonful
  castor sugar
a tablespoonful each
  of sultanas and of
  chopped citron

Grease your soufflé dish with butter, and line the sides with stale Savoy biscuits — or failing these, stale sponge cakes cut in thin slices lengthways; arrange at the bottom of the mould a layer of the sultanas, mixed with the chopped citron, cherries and angelica, and on this place the ratafias broken small and any trimmings left over from the Savoy biscuits or sponge cakes.

Beat together the eggs, extra yolks and sugar, and when the sugar is dissolved, beat in the milk slowly, and strain into the mould.

You may now either cover with buttered paper and steam gently for an hour, or place in a not too fierce oven and bake for a similar length of time.

Serve with whipped cream, or with a little apricot jam warmed.

CREMA DI BAGNOMARIA

Rich steamed custard

TO SERVE 6

2 eggs, plus 4
  extra egg yolks
½ pint milk
butter for greasing
  dish

3 tablespoonsful
  castor sugar
grated rind of half
  a lemon — alterna-
  tively, a teaspoon
  of vanilla

Grate the lemon rind into the milk, or alternatively add the vanilla and allow it to stand for half an hour. Break the eggs and extra yolks into a basin, and beat together with the sugar, then add the milk gradually. When thoroughly mixed, pass through a fine sieve, removing all the froth that has formed in the beating. Place the liquid in a greased soufflé dish and place this in a double-boiler, or if one is not available, place it on an inverted sandwich cake tin, in a saucepan of boiling water, with the water reaching to within 1½ inches from the top of the outside of the soufflé dish. Cook on top of the stove, keeping the water just under boiling point for about an hour. If you propose eating this dish hot, allow to stand for about ten minutes after it has finished cooking, before serving. Alternatively it may be allowed to become cold, when it makes a delicious cold sweet.

CROSTINI ALL'ANANASSO
Pineapple toast
TO SERVE 4

This is a dish worth trying when South African pineapples are available at reasonable prices.

- 1 or 2 of these small pineapples
- 4 ozs. butter
- a few teaspoonsful of maraschino or kirsch
- 4 ozs. sugar
- 12 thin slices of bread with the crusts removed, and cut in two lengthways
- a little apricot jam
- ½ wineglassful of water

Heat the butter in a heavy pan and in it fry the bread very lightly, not so much browning it as allowing it to absorb the butter. Previously, peel the pineapples and cut into as many slices as there are pieces of bread, lay these in a plate, sprinkle lightly with sugar and with the liqueur and allow it to stay for two or three hours. When the pineapple has 'marinated' and the bread is cooked, arrange in a flat fireproof dish, with a piece of pineapple on each piece of bread.

Cook the sugar with the water until it begins to colour, and to this add the liquid in which the pineapple has marinated, together with the apricot jam; boil together for a few minutes, then pass through a sieve and serve boiling hot over the 'crostini'.

MERINGUES

Since so many of the foregoing recipes call for 'extra yolks' a recipe for meringues is useful for employing the whites left over.

Light the oven before starting to make the meringues, and it should be a very slow oven (250 degrees at most).

> 4 egg whites
> a pinch of salt
> 1 cup castor sugar
> ½ teaspoon vanilla, if liked

Beat the egg whites with a beater, together with the pinch of salt until they are stiff and dry; now add half the sugar a little at a time, beating thoroughly after each addition; beat in the vanilla; the balance of the sugar should be folded in with a spatula or fork.

Meanwhile run some sheets of brown paper under the cold water tap and use as linings for flat 'cookie' tins. Drop the egg mixture by large spoonfuls on to the paper, place them in the oven and allow to cook for 45 to 60 minutes, or until they will lift easily from the paper. The slow cooking is essential, the trick being to dry out the mixture rather than to cook it.

When cooled, serve filled with ice cream, whipped cream, or any sweetened fruit.

PASTICCIO DI FRUTTA
Fruit flan

Prepare two pounds of mixed fruit in season, apples, apricots, plums, pears, etc. and place to cook in a stewpan with 4 ozs. granulated sugar and a wineglassful of white wine. A few soaked and stoned prunes make a welcome addition to the mixture. When the fruit is tender, add a little chopped candied citron, a couple of tablespoons of rum and a pinch of powdered cinnamon.

Meanwhile line flan tins with fairly rich pastry; pour in the fruit and bake in a hot oven until the pastry is cooked.

Serve hot or cold, with whipped cream.

SFOGLIATA DOLCE DI RICOTTA

Sfogliate are little 'bonnes-bouches' of the lightest of light puff paste, filled with various fillings; a good number are filled, as are our vol-au-vents, with minced chicken, shrimps and other savoury fillings; here is one in which ricotta cheese is suggested, but which can be made here with the substitution of cream cheese for the unobtainable ricotta.

Prepare a supply of puff pastry made of equal quantities (say 4 ozs. each) of flour and butter.

For the filling:
½ lb. cream cheese
1 tablespoonful sultanas
1 teaspoonful rum
¼ lb. castor sugar
1 tablespoonful candied orange peel
a few drops of vanilla

For the cream:
1 egg yolk
1 oz. flour
½ tablespoonful sugar
1 wineglassful milk

Beat egg and sugar for coating the sfogliate before baking. Half an hour before starting to cook, place the chopped orange peel and the sultanas in a cup with the rum, and allow them to absorb it before adding them to the mixture of cream cheese and sugar.

Combine the egg yolk, sugar and flour, gently add the milk and cook together in a double boiler till it has thickened; mix with the cheese mixture.

Divide the puff pastry into squares about 3 inches on each side; brush with beaten egg; in the centre of each plate a teaspoonful of the filling, and fold the pastry over cornerways, pressing the edges together; brush the top with beaten egg, and bake in a hot oven for twenty minutes; five minutes before finishing cooking, remove from the oven and sprinkle liberally with castor sugar, which will caramelise slightly, when the sfogliate are returned to the heat.

PIZZA

A book of Italian cookery would be incomplete without one or two recipes for this Neapolitan speciality — try it if you like; speaking for myself, the mention of pizza will always recall what arrived at my table in Naples one evening when, fancying 'something not too heavy', I ordered pizza. I waited a few moments and was then confronted with an outsize dinner plate, on which reposed something that looked rather like King Henry the Eighth's best hat made of pastry that was solid rather than light, and filled with a mixture of tomatoes and anchovies that, to say the least, was rich, and alarmingly salty. However, if it's pizza you fancy, here's how it is made.

PIZZA ALLA CAMPOFRANCO
TO SERVE 8

½ lb. plain flour
5 eggs
half tablespoon sugar
¼ lb. ham
3 tablespoons grated Parmesan
5 ozs. butter
1 teaspoon chopped basil
½ oz. brewers' yeast
½ lb. Bel Paese cheese
1 lb. tomatoes
1 tablespoon olive oil
pepper

Pile the flour on to your pastry board or cooking table, make a hollow in it and in this put the butter, two eggs, a pinch of salt and the yeast diluted with a little water or milk. Work the flour with the hands until the ingredients are absorbed, then blend in the next two eggs, and work the dough until it is elastic to the touch; then add the sugar; work the dough a little more; then place in a warmed basin. Cover with a cloth and leave in a fairly warm place for a couple of hours, by which time it should have doubled in size.

Meanwhile prepare the filling; slice the cheese, and the ham; peel the tomatoes and remove the seeds, and cook very quickly in oil so that they do not become mushy but retain their firmness.

When the dough has risen, flour your pastry board; divide the dough in two pieces, one slightly larger than the other and roll out into two circles. With the larger one, line a greased pie plate or flan tin, and on it lay first of all a layer of the cheese, then a layer of the cooked tomatoes. Season with salt and pepper and a little basil, and on this place a layer of strips of ham; continue in this way till the filling is all used up, and finish off with a layer of the grated Parmesan. Now beat the fifth egg, and with a brush paint the edges of the dough, and over it place the smaller circle of dough, pressing the edges together so that they remain closed; leave it to rise again in a warm place, for about an hour, then paint the top with the balance of the beaten egg, and cook for twenty to twenty five minutes in a hot oven. Eat hot.

Sauces

The preparation of a sauce is a ritual in Italy; it is not unusual for an Italian housewife to spend hours in loving preparation of a truly rich and enjoyable sauce to be eaten over 'pasta', and having tasted the results of some of the hours of loving labour, one has to admit the time has been well-spent.

BÉCHAMEL SAUCE

1½ ounces butter
1 pint heated milk

2 tablespoons
flour
salt and pepper

Allow butter to melt in saucepan, but before it turns brown lower heat, and blend in flour, stirring until smooth; then little by little add heated milk, stirring constantly. If liked add a pinch of nutmeg when adding the seasonings, or alternatively allow a bay leaf to remain in the sauce during its final cooking, which should be fifteen minutes from the time the milk, flour and butter are blended together. It is a good idea to use the top of a double boiler for making this sauce, placing it over the boiling water in the lower part of the boiler for the last fifteen minutes of cooking time. If it is too thick, add a little more milk from time to time.

If you have used a bay leaf for flavouring, remove before serving.

If the sauce is made well in advance, cover with a lid to prevent a skin forming.

VARIATIONS OF BÉCHAMEL SAUCE

Cheese Sauce

Make sauce as directed for plain Béchamel sauce, and when cooked, add six to eight tablespoons grated Parmesan cheese and blend well before serving.

Excellent over cooked broccoli or cauliflower.

Egg and Parsley Sauce

To 1 pint of Béchamel sauce made as directed, allow two hard boiled eggs and three tablespoons finely chopped fresh parsley, stir in just before serving. A variation is to add also a teaspoonful of finely chopped mint.

Excellent with broccoli, cauliflower or fish dishes.

Mushroom Sauce

While your Béchamel sauce is cooking, wash and chop finely ¼ lb. mushrooms and cook gently for ten minutes in hot olive oil before adding to the Béchamel.

Shrimp Sauce

To a pint of Béchamel sauce add half a pint of shrimps, shelled and chopped, and serve when heated through.
   A good sauce with fish.

BROWN SAUCE

- 1 small onion chopped finely
- 2 tablespoons chopped parsley
- 1 pint beef stock
- 4 tablespoons flour
- 1 bay leaf
- 3 tablespoons olive oil
- freshly ground black pepper
- 1 teaspoon oregano, or, failing this, ¼ teaspoon thyme

Heat oil in heavy pan, brown onion in this, with parsley, and stir in flour. When brown and blended add slowly your beef stock; allow to boil for two or three minutes, and add seasonings.

VARIATIONS OF BROWN SAUCE

Mushroom Sauce

To half a pint of brown sauce made as above, add quarter of a pound of mushrooms that have been washed, chopped finely and cooked for five minutes in hot olive oil. Delicious with steak and baked meats.

White Wine Sauce

To half a pint of brown sauce add a quarter of a pint of white wine; heat together to boiling point and serve immediately. A good sauce with baked meat.

PARSLEY BUTTER

1 tablespoon butter
1 teaspoon lemon juice
1 tablespoon finely minced parsley
pinch salt

Steak is greatly enhanced with little dabs of this simple sauce.
Cream butter and blend in remaining ingredients, mixing well and allowing to become very cold before serving at table with steak.

Variations of Parsley Butter

Instead of a tablespoon of parsley, try the combination of a teaspoonful each of mint, parsley and sweet basil, chopped finely, or alternatively, two teaspoons parsley to one of mint, or two teaspoons parsley to one of basil.

ALMOND SAUCE

2 tablespoons butter
juice of two lemons
2 ozs. blanched chopped almonds

Brown butter slightly, and slowly add chopped almonds and lemon juice. Serve hot or cold with fish.

'SOFFRITTO' OR 'BATTUTO'

This is the name given to the foundation from which stews and soups are often started; in its simplest form it consists of hot oil, butter or dripping, in which has been browned a chopped onion or a clove of garlic crushed, but it can be elaborated by the addition of chopped carrot, parsley and celery, but all very finely chopped and browned before the addition of the meat or game which is to form the stew or soup.

SIMPLE TOMATO SAUCE

- 1 medium size tin tomatoes
- 2 onions, chopped finely
- 1 teaspoon finely chopped basil, or if not available, finely chopped parsley
- 4 tablespoons olive oil
- $\frac{1}{2}$ teaspoon granulated sugar
- salt and freshly ground black pepper to taste

Heat oil in a heavy pan, fry onion until transparent and pale yellow, add parsley or basil. Strain tomatoes and add. Cook for $\frac{3}{4}$ of an hour, stirring frequently, add sugar and seasonings, and cook gently for a further ten minutes.

A good sauce to be used with rice or spaghetti.

UNSWEETENED TOMATO SAUCE

This sauce, which uses the tomato purée instead of the tinned tomatoes, needs slightly longer cooking to ensure that the too sharp flavour of the concentrated purée is somewhat diluted.

- 2 tablespoons tomato purée
- 1 clove garlic, crushed
- ½ teaspoon oregano, or failing this, ¼ teaspoon thyme
- 3 tablespoons olive oil
- 2 good-sized onions, sliced
- 1 pint water
- salt and pepper to taste

Heat oil and in it fry onion gently, until transparent and yellow-coloured; add purée, and cook together two or three minutes, stirring constantly. Add seasonings and water, cover and cook slowly for an hour or slightly more, stirring from time to time and adding more water if it becomes too thick. Serve very hot.

TOMATO SAUCE ALLA NAPOLITANA

SUFFICIENT FOR SPAGHETTI FOR 4

- 1 lb. tomatoes
- 2 stalks celery
- a few leaves of fresh basil
- 1 onion
- 1 carrot
- pepper and salt to taste

Wash tomatoes, cut in pieces and place in saucepan with other vegetables cut coarsely. Allow to cook slowly for half an hour or until the vegetables are tender. Remove from fire and pass through a sieve. Season with pepper and salt. Usually in Naples a knob of fresh lard is added at the end of the cooking and mixed well with the sauce, and just before serving a little freshly chopped basil makes an excellent finishing touch.

TOMATO SAUCE — TO ENRICH

Try the addition of a slice of ham, finely chopped, and/or a glass of Marsala to the finished sauce.

WHITE WINE SAUCE TO SERVE WITH FISH

¾ cup of the liquor in which fish has cooked
¼ cup cream
¼ cup white wine
1½ ozs. butter creamed and made into a paste with a tablespoonful of flour

Place liquor and wine in a saucepan and bring to the boil; add flour and butter paste slowly, and allow to cook for five minutes, by the end of which time the sauce will have thickened. Add cream, stirring all the while. Remove from heat and stir in a further ounce of butter a little at a time, meanwhile beating the sauce with an egg whisk.

PIQUANT SAUCE

just under ½ cup wine vinegar
¾ cup cold water
black pepper
1 teaspoonful meat extract
½ teaspoonful tomato paste
½ oz. butter
1 teaspoonful flour
½ teaspoonful French mustard
a few finely chopped capers
1 tablespoonful finely chopped parsley
a pinch of cayenne pepper

Place vinegar in a saucepan together with a fairly generous shaking of freshly ground black pepper, and a pinch of cayenne. Bring to boil and allow to cook until the vinegar is reduced by one-half. Add cold water in which you have dissolved the meat extract and the tomato paste (do not overload the sauce with tomato paste, keep the quantity small) and allow to cook together for ten or twelve minutes; strain through a fine sieve; replace on stove and re-heat. Cream the butter, and to it add the flour and when the sauce has reached the boil, reduce heat and add the butter and flour paste little by little, stirring with a wooden spoon until the sauce thickens. Cook slowly for five minutes longer, then remove from the fire and add chopped capers and chopped parsley.

Excellent with game, pigeons, etc.

SALSA OLANDESE
Hollandaise Sauce

juice of half a lemon	2 unbeaten egg yolks
$\frac{1}{4}$ lb. butter	$\frac{1}{4}$ teaspoon salt
a dash of cayenne	

An excellent sauce to serve with artichokes or asparagus.

Add lemon juice to unbeaten egg yolks. Divide butter into three and add one-third also to egg yolks. Cook over hot, but not boiling, water, stirring constantly with a wooden spoon until the butter has melted and the sauce has thickened. Add the second third of the butter and continue stirring until it has melted and the sauce has thickened again; repeat the process with the remaining third of the butter, and continue stirring until the sauce has the consistency of mayonnaise. Add the seasonings and beat sauce with a wire whip until it takes on a shiny appearance — about half a minute's beating will be needed. It should not curdle, but if it should, beat in a little boiling water until it is smooth.

TUNNY FISH SAUCE
FOR 1 POUND OF SPAGHETTI

1—6 ozs. tin tunny fish	1 lb. (or 1 medium sized tin) tomatoes
3 tablespoons chopped parsley	3 anchovies
1 tablespoon chopped capers	3 tablespoons olive oil
salt and pepper	1 clove garlic crushed

Heat the oil and in it allow the capers and crushed garlic to cook a few minutes, but do not brown; add tomatoes (cut up, skinned and seeded if raw — strained through a sieve if tinned), and cook for a further half hour. Flake tunny fish small, and chop anchovies finely and add to the tomato sauce, together with salt and pepper. Cook uncovered until it has become thick.

CLAM SAUCE

Substituting a medium sized tin of clams (drained) for the tunny fish and anchovies of the preceding recipe you have a favourite sauce for spaghetti frequently met with in and around Naples, except that there the clams come direct out of the sea and not out of tins.

SHRIMP SAUCE

1 pint (before shellings) shrimps or prawns	2 tablespoons olive oil
1 tablespoon chopped parsley	1 small onion

Chop onion and cook without browning in the heated oil, adding a tablespoonful of chopped parsley, and the shelled shrimps, together with warm water to cover and simmer 20 minutes. The addition of a few finely chopped toasted almonds is interesting.

SALSA ALLA PIZZAIOLA

- 1 tablespoon olive oil
- 6 good sizes tomatoes
- 2 or 3 crushed cloves garlic
- 1 tablespoon fresh oregano, basil or parsley

Heat the oil and allow crushed garlic to cook gently in it, but do not allow it to brown. Add peeled and cut up tomatoes, pepper and salt and cook fairly fast until tomatoes are cooked through but not reduced to a pulp. Add a good tablespoonful of oregano, basil or parsley, and before serving add another clove of garlic cut very, very fine.

Tinned tomatoes may be used if fresh are not available, but for this sauce the fresh are infinitely preferable.

An excellent sauce to serve with beefsteak.

SALSA VERDE
Green sauce

- a good handful of parsley
- 2 anchovies
- 1 small cooked potato
- 1 small onion cut fine
- 1 tablespoonful capers
- 1 small gherkin
- 1 clove garlic, crushed
- salt, pepper and oil
- a tablespoonful of wine vinegar

Pound together in a heavy mortar all the ingredients except the oil and vinegar until they form a paste. Slowly add sufficient oil to render this to the consistency of mayonnaise, finally blend in a tablespoonful of wine vinegar, and serve very cold. A little fresh bread crumb may be substituted for the boiled potato.

PESTO
FOR 2 PEOPLE

Pesto is a sauce of Genoese origin that finds its ways into many dishes; it is excellent with spaghetti, for instance, and a tablespoon added to minestrone greatly enhances the flavour. Any left-over pesto may be placed in a small jar, covered with olive oil and kept for some days.

- 3 cloves garlic
- sufficient fresh basil to produce 3 tablespoons when removed from stalks and torn into small pieces
- about 2 tablespoons fresh olive oil
- 1 cup grated Sardo cheese, but since this Sardinian cheese made of ewes' milk is not easy to procure, Parmesan may be substituted

Pound the garlic and basil to a paste in a mortar, add the cheese and continue pounding until a thick paste results, then slowly add oil until you have a mixture the consistency of mayonnaise.

A few almonds, pine nuts or even walnuts pounded into the paste make an interesting variation.

RAGÙ BOLOGNESE
SUFFICIENT FOR 6

No book on Italian cookery would be complete without a recipe for this, one of Italy's most famous sauces. ½ lb. lean beef, or a mixture of beef with veal and/or pork, though the beef should predominate, and all should be passed through a mincer twice.

1½ ozs. butter	1½ cups stock or water, or for preference 1 cup stock plus ½ cup white wine
3 ozs. streaky bacon	
onion, carrot, a stick of celery, a crushed clove garlic	
	1 teaspoon tomato paste
2 or 3 cloves or a pinch of powdered cloves	¼ cup cream
	salt and pepper to taste

A few chopped mushrooms may be added if liked, and if you have three or four chicken livers available, these, chopped, are a great improvement.

Having minced the meat, place in a stewpan with the heated butter, add chopped bacon, onion, carrot and celery, all of which can, to save time, have been passed through the mincer. Add two or three dried cloves or a pinch of powered cloves, and allow to cook until the meat has browned and the vegetables are a golden colour. Add the stock and/or wine little by little, add tomato paste moistened with a little stock, stir well; add salt and pepper. Cover meat with the liquid, lower heat and allow the mixture to cook gently for another 15 minutes. In one of the traditional recipes milk is used instead of stock, which results in a richer-tasting sauce, but this is purely a matter of personal preference.

At the end of the cooking time add the cream and mix well. Excellent sauce for serving with spaghetti.

LIVER SAUCE FOR GNOCCHI

½ lb. liver, (calves' liver will do, but chicken livers are preferable)
½ pint chicken stock
2 ozs. butter
¼ lb. button mushrooms
1 glass white wine (half a cupful)
1 tablespoon flour

Chop and flour liver, chop mushrooms small, and sauté both in butter in a heavy pan for 10 to 12 minutes, season with salt and pepper, stir in any balance of flour, and slowly add the wine; allow to cook 7 or 8 minutes longer before adding the stock. Simmer until thick.

APPLE SAUCE

4 cooking apples, medium size
1 teaspoonful lemon juice
1 coffee-spoonful grated lemon rind

Peel apples, cut them into small pieces and place in a stewpan with water to cover, and allow to cook until they can be mashed into a purée. Add grated lemon rind and a pinch of salt, remove from heat, and stir in lemon juice and mix well. Serve with roast pork.

BREAD SAUCE

½ pint milk
1 medium sized onion stuck with cloves (4 of these)
white bread
½ oz. butter
salt
cayenne pepper

Place the onion stuck with cloves and the milk in a saucepan and bring to the boil, allow to cook slowly for five minutes, then remove the onion and add enough white breadcrumbs to make a fairly thick sauce; mix well; remove from stove and stir in the butter and, if available, a tablespoonful of cream.

For serving with roast chicken.

MAYONNAISE

Legend has it that a certain Duke of Mayenne, a great gourmet, was so busy discussing with the camp chef the preparation of a special sauce to grace a cold chicken that by the time the discussion had come to an end, his own cavalry had been overcome by those of the enemy, and the Battle of Arques was lost for his side. So much for history; the Duke deserves an honourable mention, for the sauce that caused the trouble was the forerunner of Mayonnaise, and took its name from the unfortunate gentleman who had a hand in its creation.

For a good mayonnaise you will need:

1¼ cups good olive oil
a pinch of salt

3 egg yolks
about 3 teaspoons lemon juice or wine vinegar

Place the egg yolks and a pinch of salt in a bowl and with a wooden spoon or a metal egg whisk beat them slowly, slowly until thick, and then start adding your olive oil, literally drop by drop. After two or three tablespoonsful have added, the mayonnaise may be a trifle too thick, in which case beat in a little lemon juice or wine vinegar. Continue beating and adding oil slowly until the desired consistency is obtained.

SALSA REMOULADE

To a mayonnaise made as in the foregoing recipe add the following:

1 tablespoonful made mustard — or to taste	1 tablespoonful finely chopped parsley
2 tablespoonfuls finely chopped capers	2 or 3 chopped gherkins

Excellent to serve with cold meat or with shellfish.

DRESSING FOR GREEN SALAD
SUFFICIENT FOR SALAD FOR 4

½ teaspoon salt	1 teaspoon castor sugar
1 teaspoon French mustard	freshly ground black pepper
1 tablespoon wine vinegar	3 tablespoons olive oil

Mix together all ingredients except the oil, then slowly add the oil, and mix till well blended. An excellent mixer is of the type sold for mixing such drinks as Horlicks or Ovaltine. The mixing time is two or three minutes, and the dressing is all the better if it is made an hour in advance of the meal at which it is to be used. Once blended it can be embellished by the addition of a teaspoonful or more of finely chopped parsley, mint or basil, and by half a clove of garlic very finely chopped, if liked. DO NOT ADD TO YOUR SALAD UNTIL A MOMENT OR TWO BEFORE SERVING.

CHICKEN SAUCE
TO SERVE 4

½ pint of cream
2 ozs. Bel Paese cheese
¼ lb. cream cheese

6 ozs. cooked breast of chicken cut in dice
¼ lb. mushrooms
2 ozs. butter

Place cream and cheese in a double boiler and cook slowly over hot water, stirring constantly until the mixture is smooth and creamy. Meanwhile, sauté the chopped mushrooms in the butter. Add these and the chopped chicken to the sauce; mix well and serve hot over any kind of pasta asciutta. Grated Parmesan cheese sprinkled over the finished dish is an improvement.

PEA SAUCE
To serve with macaroni or with rice

1 onion chopped finely
1 rasher of streaky bacon
½ pint chicken stock
salt and pepper to taste

3 tablespoons olive oil
1 lb. peas (before shelling)
1 tablespoon parsley chopped fine

Heat olive oil in heavy pan, and in it cook the onion until it is golden colour; cut bacon small and add, allowing it to cook for three or four minutes. Add stock, peas and seasoning, and cook slowly for fifteen or twenty minutes.

HAM SAUCE WITH CREAM
TO SERVE 4

4 ozs. lean ham or cooked gammon cut small

2 ozs. butter
½ pint cream

Melt the butter in a heavy pan, add the ham or gammon and allow to brown slightly before adding the cream. Lower heat, and cook together until the mixture begins to bubble. This sauce is delicious served over freshly cooked pasta of any variety.

MUSHROOM AND TOMATO
SAUCE
SUFFICIENT FOR 6 PEOPLE

1 lb. mushrooms
1 medium-size tin tomatoes
3 tablespoons olive oil
1 clove garlic — crushed
cayenne pepper to taste
1 tablespoon chopped basil, or if not available an equal quantity of finely chopped mint or parsley
a pinch of chopped thyme
a pinch of salt

Heat oil and in it allow the crushed garlic to brown; add mushrooms, sliced finely and simmer for ten minutes; pass tomatoes through a sieve, and add to the sauce together with the remaining ingredients. Cover and allow to cook very slowly for an hour, stirring from time to time. Serve very hot as a sauce with any type of pasta.

MEAT SAUCE
FOR SERVING OVER SPAGHETTI

- 2 tablespoons tomato purée
- 1 clove garlic, crushed
- 1 cup dry white wine
- 1 bay leaf
- salt and pepper
- 2 tablespoons olive oil
- 1½ cups warm water
- 1 onion, chopped fine
- ½ lb. lean beef passed twice through mincer

Heat oil and in it brown onion and garlic and meat, add tomato paste and cook for a further five minutes before adding pepper, salt, bay leaf, water and wine. Cover and allow to cook slowly for one hour, stirring from time to time; remove bay leaf and cook a few minutes longer before serving with spaghetti.

MEAT SAUCE WITH MUSHROOMS

- ½ lb. lean beef passed twice through mincer
- 2 tablespoons olive oil
- 1 tablespoon tomato purée
- pinch cayenne
- ¼ lb. mushrooms, washed and sliced thinly
- 1 clove garlic, crushed
- 1 medium size tin tomatoes
- pepper and salt

Heat oil in heavy pan, add mushrooms, garlic, cayenne, meat and simmer for five minutes; strain tomatoes and add, simmer gently for ¾ of an hour, blend tomato purée with a little water, add to first mixture, together with salt, cover and cook slowly a further 30 minutes, stirring from time to time. Keep hot till time to use.

[215]

CAPER SAUCE
TO BE SERVED HOT WITH ANY FISH

2 tablespoons capers
1 tablespoon flour
1 tablespoon
 chopped parsley
salt and pepper

2 ozs. butter
2 tablespoons wine
 vinegar
$\frac{1}{4}$ pint beef stock

Drain capers and chop finely; heat butter in heavy pan, add flour, stirring until it is smooth and has turned a golden brown; stir in capers, add vinegar slowly, and finally stir in parsley and seasoning, finishing up with the beef stock. Simmer for quarter of an hour and serve hot.

SWEET SOUR SAUCE
FOR SERVING WITH VEGETABLES OR WITH FISH DISHES

$\frac{1}{4}$ lb. granulated
 sugar
1 tablespoon flour
2 tablespoons wine
 vinegar

$\frac{1}{4}$ pint hot water
$\frac{1}{2}$ pint stock
salt and pepper

Brown sugar in heavy pan, sprinkle flour over and blend together; add hot water slowly, following with stock, vinegar and seasonings. Allow to cook 2 or 3 minutes and serve hot.

SWEET SOUR SAUCE WITH NUTS
TO SERVE WITH MEAT OR GAME

- ¾ lb. chopped nuts, preferably almonds or pine nuts
- 2 squares unsweetened chocolate
- 2 tablespoons granulated sugar
- ¼ pint wine vinegar
- 3 tablespoons red currant jelly
- 2 tablespoons sultanas
- the grated rind of half a lemon and half an orange
- ½ pint stock

Allow sugar to caramelise slightly in heavy pan before stirring in grated chocolate and other ingredients. Simmer for half an hour, seasoning with pepper and salt to taste.

YET ANOTHER SWEET-SOUR SAUCE
TO SERVE WITH MEATS

- 2 tablespoons butter
- pinch salt
- 2 tablespoons wine vinegar
- 2 tablespoons flour
- ½ pint stock or hot water in which vegetables have been cooked
- 2 tablespoons gran. sugar
- fresh ground black pepper

Caramelise sugar and blend in flour, adding slowly the rest of the ingredients, and cook together slowly for twenty minutes before serving.

TUNNY SAUCE WITH BLACK OLIVES
TO SERVE 4

4 ozs. black olives
6 or 8 anchovies
tomato sauce —
   (see any of the
   various recipes
   for this under
   'SAUCES')

1 medium sized tin of tunny fish

Having prepared your tomato sauce, stone and chop the olives, mash the tunny and anchovies, and add to the sauce while it is still cooking; mix well, and serve hot over fresh cooked pasta.

MARINARA SAUCE
TO SERVE 4

1 medium sized onion
4 tablespoons olive oil
½ pint white wine
1 pint shrimps

1 clove garlic, crushed
6 tomatoes, peeled
½ teaspoon brown sugar
salt and pepper to taste

Heat the oil in a heavy pan and in it cook the chopped onion and crushed garlic until golden colour; add tomatoes, cut small, together with sugar and pepper and salt. Lower heat and allow to cook gently for 20 minutes. While this is cooking, peel shrimps, and add them together with the wine to the tomato mixture, cooking gently together for 15 minutes. A little chopped fresh basil may be added 5 minutes before the end of the cooking time, or failing this, chopped parsley.

Serve hot over pasta of any type.

A VENETIAN SAUCE FOR FISH

2½ ozs. butter
½ cupful each of meat (preferably chicken) and fish stock

1 tablespoon flour
salt and pepper
green colouring

Place half the butter in a small saucepan and allow to melt but not to brown; blend in the flour, and very slowly add meat and fish stock, stirring all the time until thick. Lower heat and add the remainder of the butter, a very little knob at a time, and when all used up and the sauce is thick remove from the fire, stir in the green colouring and serve.

ANCHOVY SAUCE

10 to 12 anchovy fillets pounded to a paste
1 clove garlic — crushed
yolks of 4 hard-boiled eggs

2 tablespoons tarragon vinegar
2 tablespoons best olive oil
4 tablespoons parsley, chopped fine

Heat oil in a heavy pan, add pounded anchovies and crushed garlic, and cook slowly for five minutes; add parsley, vinegar and pounded egg yolks, stirring constantly until well blended. Remove from fire and serve very cold. A good sauce to serve with cold meats or fish.

Index

Agnello arrosto, 137
Agnello in casseruola, 138
Agnolotti, 67
Almond sauce, 201
Anchovies, 15
Anchovies and tunny fish with tagliatelle, 55
Anchovies with fried bread, 26
Anchovies with spaghetti, 61
Anchovy sauce, 219
Anchovy toast, 24
Anguilla alla Ferrarese, 106
Anolini, 67
Antipasti, cold, 20 *ff*.
Antipasti, hot, 23 *ff*.
Antipasto, fennel, 22, 23
Antipasto Fortunata Ruocco's, 23
Antipasto, pepper (cold), 23
Antipasto, pepper (hot), 25
Antipasto, rice, 21
Apple charlotte, 190
Apple fritters, 186
Apple sauce, 210
Apricot fritters, 186
Aragosta lessata, 104
Arangini, 86
Aringa alla gratella, 107
Artichoke omelette, 97
Artichokes, 163—4
Artichokes, fricassee of, 163
Artichokes, Jewish, 164
Artichokes stewed with peas, 164
Artichokes with liver, 144
Asparagi alla Milanese, 165
Asparagi all'olio, 165
Asparagus Milanese style, 165
Asparagus with oil, 165
Aubergines Genoese style, 169
Aubergines Neapolitan style, 170
Aubergines stuffed, 170

Baccala, cream of, 110

Bacon and sausage ravioli filling, 71
Basil, 12
Batter, fritter, 185
Battuto, 202
Batuffoli al sugo, 91
Bay, 12
Bean soup, haricot, 43
Beans, broad, with bacon, 168
Beans, French, buttered, 165
Beans, French, fricassee, 166
Beans, French, Roman style, 166
Beans, haricot or butter, with fish, 22
Beccacce al salmi, 158
Beccacce alla Romagnola, 159
Béchamel sauce, 199
Beef, domestic style, 131
Beef, stewed, 130
Beef, Trieste style, 130
Bel Paese, 14
Bodino di gabinetto, 191
Bodino di latte alla mandorle, 191
Borage, 13
Braciuole ripiene, 150
Braciuole di vitello alla Veronese, 135
Brains risotto, 79
Brains rissoles, 148
Brains Tuscan style, 149
Breadcrumbs, 13
Bread, fried, with anchovies, 26
Bread, fried, with cheese cream, 26
Bread, fried, see also *Pandorato alla Romana* sauce, 210
Broad beans with bacon, 168
Broccoli strascicati, 176
Broccoli with macaroni, 62
Broccoli with salt pork, 176
Brown sauce, 200

Brussels sprouts served with chestnuts, 175
Butter beans with fish, 22

Cabinet pudding, 191
Cacciucco alla Toscana, 103
Calamaretti, 105
Cannelloni, 49
Cannelloni filled with cheese and sausage, 66
Caper sauce, 216
Cappelletti, 67
Cappelletti in brodo, 71
Cappon magro, 125
Capretto in casseruola, 138
Carciofi, 163—4
Carciofi alla giudaica, 164
Carciofi in fricassea, 163
Carciofi in umido con piselli, 164
Carote al burro, 174
Carp, 123
Carrots, buttered, 174
Carrots, candied, 175
Carrots, cooked in butter, 175
Cauliflower Sicilian style, 176
Cauliflower with meat sauce, 176
Cavolfiore alla lionese, 176
Cavolfiore alla Siciliana, 176
Ceci, 92
Ceci alla marinara, 93
Celery, 13
Celery, stuffed, 22
Charlotte di mele, pere o pesche, 190
Cheese, 14
Cheese, cream, 27
Cheese, dishes, 94 *ff.*
Cheese, fried, 100
Cheese, omelette, 96
Cheese, ravioli filling, 69
Cheese, rice balls, 85
Cheese, sauce, 199

Cheese and onion soup, 42, 43
Chestnut fritters, 188
Chestnut purée, 177
Chestnut soup, 39
Chick peas, 92
Chick peas, sailors' style, 93
Chicken, 152 *ff.*
Chicken, breasts, Lombard style, 155
Chicken, broth, 31
Chicken, garnished, 153
Chicken in white wine, 155
Chicken, liver tartlets, 24
Chicken, livers and rice soufflé, 89
Chicken, purée, 156
Chicken, ravioli filling, 70
Chicken, risotto, 80
Chicken, Roman style, 156
Chicken, sauce, 213
Chicken, stew, 152
Chicken, tartlets, 24
Chicken with cream, 154
Chicken with olives, 152
Chicken with peas, 153
Chicken with mushrooms, 154
Cinnamon, 18
Cipolle ripiene, 171
Clam sauce, 206
Clams fishermen's style, 122
Clams with eggs, 121
Cloves, 18
Cod *au gratin,* 103
Cod, Florentine style, 108
Cod, salt, creamed, 110
Cod, salt, in sauce, 109
Cod, salt, Ligurian style, 109
Cod, salt, rissoles of, 111
Cod with tomatoes, 108
Coniglio alla borghese, 160
Coniglio in salsa piccante, 160, 161
Cooking temperatures, 11

Cooking times for *pasta*, 51
Coriander seeds, 18
Coscia di manzo alla casalinga, 131
Costolette di vitello al sugo, 134
Costolette Milanese, 133
Crabs, soft shell, 105
Crawfish, 105
Cream cheese ravioli filling, 69
Cream of mushroom soup, 44
Cream of tomato soup, 44
Crema di bagnomaria, 192
Crostini all'ananasso, 193
Crostini alla Napolitana, 27
Cucumber salad, 182
Custard, rich steamed, 192

Eels Ferrara style, 106
Eels, roast, 106, 107
Eels, stewed, 107
Egg dishes, 94 *ff*.
Egg and parsley sauce, 199
Eggs, hard boiled, and salad, 182, 183
Eggs, scrambled, with cheese, 99
Eggs with rice, 99
Elbow macaroni pie, 57

Fagiano al Madera, 159
Fagioli alla provinciale, 167
Fagiolini al burro, 165
Fagiolini alla Romana, 166
Fagiolini in fricassea, 166
Fave al gunciale, 168
Fegato alla Milanese, 143
Fegato alla Spagnola, 141
Fegato alla Toscana, 143
Fegato alla Veneziana, 144
Fegato all' Italiana, 142
Fegato, flan di, 145
Fegato, polpette di, 145

Fennel, 14

Fennel, *antipasto*, 22
Fennel, seeds, 18
Fennel, stuffed, 22
Fettucine with meat sauce and cheese, 56
Fig fritters, 187
Finocchiona, see Fennel seeds
Fish, 101 *ff*.
Fish *au gratin*, 102
Fish cakes, 103
Fish, Genoese style, 115
Fish in paper cases, 118
Fish, mixed fried, 121
Fish salad, 125
Fish, Sicilian fried, 102
Fish soup, see Soups, fish
Fish, tinned and salted, 15
Fish, to boil, 119
Fish, to roast, 119
Fish with haricot or butter beans, 22
Flavourings, 12—19
Fortunata Ruocco's cold pepper antipasto, 23
French beans, buttered, 165
French beans, fricassee, 166
French beans, Roman style, 166
Fricassee of artichokes, 163
Fricassee, French beans, 166
Fricassee, rabbit, 161
Fricassee, veal, 136
Frittata ai carciofi, 97
Frittata ai funghi, 96
Frittata ai legumi, 96
Frittata ai prosciutto, 97
Frittata ai tartuffi, 95
Frittata al formaggio, 96
Frittata alla cipolle, 97
Frittata alla salsa di pomidoro, 96
Frittata col riso, 98
Frittata di patate, 98
Frittata farcita, 97

Frittata semplice, 95
Frittelle alla Fiorentina, 188
Fritters, 185 *ff*.
Fritters, apple, 186
Fritters, apricot, 186
Fritters, batter for, 185
Fritters, chestnut, 188
Fritters, fig, 187
Fritters, Florentine, 188
Fritters, peach, 187
Fritters, pear, 186
Fritters, plum, 187
Fritters, semolina, 187
Fritters, sweet, 189
Fritto misto mare, 121
Frogs, 127—8
Fruit flan, 194

Game, 156 *ff*
Gardener's wife's salad, 183
Garlic, 15
Garlic, soup, 42
Gavatoni, 51
Genoese fish soup, 46
Genoese rice, 80
Gnocchi, 67, 71 *ff*.
Gnocchi, *alla Romana*, 73
Gnocchi, potato, 72
Gnocchi, semolina, 72
Gnocchi with tomato sauce, 73
Green sauce, 207
Grey mullet, grilled, 124

Ham omelette, 97
Ham, sauce with cream, 213
Ham with spaghetti, 59
Hare in sweet sour sauce, 157
Hare, stew, 157
Haricot bean soup, 43
Haricot beans, 167
Haricot beans with bacon, 167
Haricot beans with fish, 22
Herbs, 12—19

Herbs, omelette with, 95
Herrings, grilled, 107
Hollandaise sauce, 205

Insalata alla giardiniera, 183

Juniper berries, 15

Kid, pot roast of, 138
Kidneys, Bolognese style, 148
Kidneys, stewed, 147

Lamb, pot roast of, 138
Lamb, roast, 137
Lasagne, 49
Lasagne al forno, 64
Lasagne imbottite, 65
Lasagne verdi, 63
Lentil soup, 34, 36
Lettuce salad, 182
Lettuce soup, 41
Lingua alla salsa, 149
Lingua con olive, 150
Liver flan, 145
Liver flan, Italian style, 142
Liver flan, Milanese style, 143
Liver flan, rissoles, 145
Liver flan, sauce, 210
Liver flan, Spanish style, 141
Liver flan, Tuscan style, 143
Liver flan, Venetian style, 144
Liver flan with artichokes, 144
Lobster, boiled, 104
Lobster, cold, 104
Lobster, fried, 105

Macaroni, 49
Macaroni, baked with cheese, 58
Macaroni, baked with sour cream, 59
Macaroni, pie, elbow, 57
Macaroni with broccoli, 62
Manzo alla massaia, 131

[226]

Manzo alla Triestina, 130
Manzo in umido, 130
Marinara sauce, 218
Marjoram, 15
Marrow, baby, fried, 177
Marrow, baby, stewed, 178
Marrow, soup *alla Napolitana*, 41
Marrow, stuffed, 178
Marrow with tomato, 179
Marrows, 177
Mayonnaise, 211
Meat balls, 35
Meat balls with spaghetti, 56
Meat ravioli filling, 70
Meat sauce, 215
Meat sauce with mushrooms, 215
Meats, 129 *ff.*
Melanzane alla Genovese, 169
Melanzane alla Napolitana, 170
Melanzane ripiene, 170
Meringues, 194
Merluzzo alla Fiorentina, 108
Merluzzo in salsa, 108
Milk pudding with almonds, 191
Minestre Crecy, 37
Minestrone, 32, 33
Mint, 15
Mont Blanc, 189
Mozzarella, 14
Mullet, grey, grilled, 124
Mullet, red, 124
Mullet, red, fried, 114
Mullet, red, Leghorn style, 114
Mullet, red, Ligurian style, 114
Mullet, red, Trieste style, 115
Mushroom omelette, 96
Mushroom risotto, 77
Mushroom sauce (brown), 200
Mushroom sauce (white), 200
Mushroom and tomato sauce, 214
Mushroom soup, cream of, 44
Mushrooms, dried, 16

Mushrooms, stuffed, 24
Mussels fishermen's style, 122
Mussels with eggs, 121
Myrtle, 16

Nasello con piselli, 118
Noodles, 49
Noodles, stuffed, 65
Nutmeg, 18

Olive oil, 16
Olives, fried green, 28
Omelettes, 94 *ff.*
Omelette, artichoke, 97
Omelette, cheese, 96
Omelette, ham, 97
Omelette, herb, 95
Omelette, mushroom, 96
Omelette, onion, 97
Omelette, plain, 95
Omelette, potato, 98
Omelette, rice, 98
Omelette, stuffed, 97
Omelette, truffle, 95
Omelette, vegetable, 96
Omelette with tomato sauce, 96
Onion and cheese soup, 42, 43
Onion omelette, 97
Onion salad, 182
Onions, stuffed, 171
Onions with tomatoes, 173
Oregano, see Marjoram
Ossobuco, 136
Ossobuco alla Milanese, 137
Ostriche alla Veneziana, 120
Oven heats, 11
Oysters Venetian style, 120

Pancakes, potato, 171
Pandorato alla crema di formaggio, 26
Pandorato alla Romana, 25
Parmesan, 14

Parsley, 16
Parsley, butter, 201
Parsley and egg sauce, 199
Partridges Milanese style, 158
Pasta, 49 *ff.*
Pasta, home made, 52
Pasta, quantities of, 52
Pasta, to cook, 50—1
Pasticcio di frutta, 194
Pastina, 49
Patate al burro, 173
Patate arrosto, 172
Patate con salsa di pomidoro, 173
Patate in stufato, 172
Pea sauce, 213
Peas, green, Parisian style, 169
Peas, green, with ham, 168
Peas, stewed with artichokes, 164
Peach charlotte, 190
Peach fritters, 187
Pear charlotte, 190
Pear fritters, 186
Pepper, 18
Pepper, *antipasto* (cold), 23
Pepper, *antipasto* (hot), 25
Perniciotte alla Milanese, 158
Pesce gratinato, 102
Pesci accartocciati, 118
Pesto, 208
Pheasant in Madeira, 159
Piccate, see *Scaloppine*
Pigeons with peas, 157
Pigs in blankets, 120
Pike, 123
Pike *au gratin*, 123
Pine nuts, 17
Pineapple toast, 193
Piquant sauce, 204
Piselli alla Parigina, 169
Piselli al prosciutto, 168
Pizza, 196
Pizza alla Campofranco, 196—7

Plum fritters, 187
Pollo ai funghi, 154
Pollo ai piselli, 153
Pollo alla crema, 154
Pollo alla Romana, 156
Pollo alle olive, 152
Pollo al vino bianco, 155
Pollo con verdure, 153
Pollo in umido, 152
Pollo, petti di, alla Lombarda, 155
Polenta, 90 *ff.*
Polenta with cheese, 91
Polenta with tomato sauce, 91
Polpetti, 35
Polpettine di stoccafisso, 111
Pomidori alla casalinga, 174
Pork chops *alla Napolitana*, 139
Pork chops with prunes, 140
Pork in milk *alla Bolognese*, 138
Pork, loin of, Perugian style, 139
Pork, loin of, Tuscan style, 139
Potato fritters, 172
Potato *gnocchi*, 72
Potato omelette, 98
Potato pancakes, 171
Potatoes, baked, 172
Potatoes, buttered, 173
Potatoes, sauteed, 172
Potatoes, with tomato sauce
Poultry, 152 *ff.*
Pozzuoli fishermen's soup, 47
Pudding, cabinet, 191
Pudding, milk, with almonds, 191
Purée of chestnuts, 177
Purée of chicken, 156

Rabbit, citizen style, 160
Rabbit, fricassee, 161
Rabbit, in piquant sauce, 160, 161
Ragù Bolognese, 209
Rane alla Gastalda, 128
Ravioli, 67 *ff.*

Ravioli, bacon and sausage filling for, 71
Ravioli, cheese filling for, 69
Ravioli, chicken filling for, 70
Ravioli, cream cheese filling for, 69
Ravioli, fillings for, 68 *ff.*
Ravioli, meat filling for, 70
Ravioli spinach filling for, 68
Ravioli, to make, 67—8
Red mullet, 124
Red mullet, fried, 114
Red mullet, Leghorn style, 113
Red mullet, Ligurian style, 114
Red mullet, Trieste style, 115
Rice, 74 *ff.*
Rice, *antipasti*, 21
Rice, boiled, with butter and cheese, 84
Rice, boiled, with butter and celery, 85
Rice, fried, with bacon and egg, 88
Rice, omelette, 98
Rice and peas Venetian style, 81
Rice, soufflé with chicken livers, 89
Rice, soufflé with shrimps, 89
Rice, to boil, 83
Rice with cabbage, 83
Rice with celery, 83
Rice with turnips, 82
Ricotta, 14
Rigatoni, 51
Risi e bisi, 81
Riso e cavoli, 83
Riso e rape, 82
Riso e sedano, 83
Riso in cagnoni, 84
Rosemary, 17
Risotto, brains, 79
Risotto, chicken, 80
Risotto, favourite, 78
Risotto, Genoese, 80
Risotto *in cagnoni di magro*, 85
Risotto, mushroom, 77
Risotto, plain, 76
Risotto, rich, 77
Risotto, shellfish, 79
Risotto, Venetian, 81
Rissoles, brains, 149
Rissoles, liver, 145
Rissoles, salt cod, 111
Rognoni alla Bolognese, 148
Rognoni in umido, 147
Rump steak housewife fashion, 131

Saffron, 17
Sage, 18
Sailors' soup, 46
Salad dressing, 212
Salads, 181 *ff.*
Salads, cucumber, 182
Salads, gardener's wife's, 183
Salads, hard boiled egg, 182, 183
Salads, lettuce, 182
Salads, mixed, 183
Salads, onion, 182
Salads, plain, 182
Salads with sour cream, 183
Salsa alla pizzaiola, 207
Salsa olandese, 205
Salsa Remoulade, 212
Salsa verde, 207
Salsiccie alla Triestina, 141
Salt, 18
Salt cod, creamed, 110
Salt cod, in sauce, 109
Salt cod, Ligurian style, 109
Salt cod, rissoles of, 111
Sardines, 15
Sartù, 87
Sauces, 198 *ff.*
Sauce, almond, 201
Sauce, anchovy, 219

Sauce, apple, 210
Sauce, Béchamel, 199
Sauce, bread, 210
Sauce, brown, 200
Sauce, caper, 216
Sauce, cheese, 199
Sauce, chicken, 213
Sauce, clam, 206
Sauce, egg and parsley, 199
Sauce, green, 207
Sauce, ham, 213
Sauce, Hollandaise, 205
Sauce, liver, 210
Sauce, marinara, 218
Sauce, meat, 215
Sauce, meat, with mushrooms, 215
Sauce, mushroom, 200
Sauce, mushroom and tomato, 214
Sauce, parsley and egg, 199
Sauce, pea, 213
Sauce, piquant, 204
Sauce, shrimp, 200, 206
Sauce, sweet sour, 216, 217
Sauce, sweet sour, with nuts, 217
Sauce, tomato, 202
Sauce, tomato, *alla Napolitana*, 203
Sauce, tomato, unsweetened, 203
Sauce, tomato and mushroom, 214
Sauce, tunny fish, 206, 218
Sauce, Venetian, 219
Sauce, white wine, 201, 204
Sausages Trieste style, 141
Sausages with tomato sauce, 141
Scaloppe alla Modenese, 134
Scaloppe di vitello al sugo, 134
Scaloppe Milanese, 133
Scaloppine al Marsala, 133
Scampi alla Lombarda, 117

Scampi alla Modenese, 117
Scampi fried, 116
Semolina fritters, 187
Semolina *gnocchi*, 187
Sfogliate dolce di ricotta, 195
Shellfish risotto, 79
Shrimp sauce, 200, 206
Shrimps and rice soufflé, 89
Sicilian fried fish, 102
Sicilian recipes for *pasta*, 61—2
Snails, 127
Soffritto, 202
Sole fried in oil, 122
Sole grilled, 103
Sole with white wine, 122
Soufflé of rice and chicken livers, 89
Soufflé of rice and shrimps, 89
Soufflé of *tagliatelle*, 54
Soup stock, clear, 30
Soups, 29 *ff*.
Soup, bean, haricot, 43
Soup, cheese and onion, 42, 43
Soup, chestnut, 39
Soup, cream of mushroom, 44
Soup, cream of tomato, 44
Soup, fish, 45 *ff*.
Soup, garlic, 42
Soup, Genoese, 46
Soup, haricot bean, 43
Soup, lentil, 34, 36
Soup, lettuce, 41
Soup, marrow, *alla Napolitana*, 41
Soup, mushroom, cream of, 44
Soup, onion and cheese, 42, 43
Soup, Pozzuoli fishermen's, 47
Soup, sailors', 46
Soup, spinach, 36, 37, 38
Soup, Syracusan, 48
Soup, tomato, cream of, 44
Soup, vegetable, 35, 40
Spaghetti, 49

Spaghetti, *con salsa di vongole*, 55
Spaghetti with anchovies, 61
Spaghetti with bacon, egg and onion, 62
Spaghetti with butter and cheese, 58
Spaghetti with clam sauce, 55
Spaghetti with fresh fennel sauce, 61
Spaghetti with green olive oil sauce, 60
Spaghetti with ham, 59
Spaghetti with meat balls, 56
Spaghetti with oil and garlic, 60
Spices, 18
Spinach ravioli filling, 68
Spinach, Roman style, 179
Spinach soup, 36, 37, 38
Spinaci alla Parmigiana, 180
Spinaci alla Piemontese, 180
Steak, stuffed, 150
Stew Florentine style, 132
Stoccafisso alla Ligure, 109
Stoccafisso in salsa, 109
Stoccafisso polpettine di, 111
Stock, 30
Stock pot, 30
Stracciatelle, 39
Stufato alla Fiorentina, 132
Stuffed meats, 150—1
Sturgeon, 124
Sturgeon, housewife style, 113
Suppli, 85
Sweet sour sauce, 216, 217
Sweet sour sauce, with nuts, 217
Sweets, 184 *ff*.

Tagliatelle, 49
Tagliatelle alla crema, 54
Tagliatelle, soufflé, 54
Tagliatelle with anchovy and tunny fish, 55

Tarragon, 18
Tench, 124
Testa di vitello alla Toscana, 148
Thyme, 19
Tomato paste, 19
Tomato sauce, 202
Tomato sauce, *alla Napolitana*, 203
Tomato sauce, to enrich, 203
Tomato sauce, unsweetened, 203
Tomato and mushroom sauce, 214
Tomato soup, cream of, 44
Tomatoes, 19
Tomatoes, housewife style, 174
Tomatoes with onions, 173
Tongue with olives, 150
Tongue with sauce, 149
Tortellini, 67
Triglie alla Ligure, 114
Triglie alla Livornese, 113
Triglie alla Triestina, 115
Trimmings, 12—19
Tripe, Florentine style, 146
Tripe, Italian style, 146
Tripe with Parmesan, 147
Trippa alla Fiorentina, 146
Trippa all' Italiana, 146
Trout, 123
Truffle omelette, 95
Tunny fish, 15
Tunny fish and anchovy with *tagliatelle*, 55
Tunny fish, Ligurian style, 112
Tunny fish, roast, 125
Tunny fish, sauce, 206, 218
Tunny fish, Sicilian style, 111
Tunny fish with peas, 111
Tunny fish with veal, 134

Uove col riso, 99
Uove stracciato al formaggio, 99

Veal, 132 ff.
Veal, chops Veronese style, 135
Veal, fricassee, 136
Veal, pie, stuffed, 151
Veal, roast, 136
Veal, stew with peas, 135
Veal with tunny fish, 134
Vegetable omelette, 96
Vegetable soup, 40
Vegetable soup with meat balls, 35
Vegetables, 162 ff.
Venetian sauce, 219
Vitello in fricassea, 136
Vitallo in umido con piselli, 135
Vitello ripieno al pasticcio, 151

Weights and measures, 10

White wine sauce, 201
White wine sauce for fish, 204
Whiting, curled, 118
Woodcock, 158, 159

Zabaglione (Zabaione), 185
Zucchini fritti, 177
Zuppa alla Foubonne, 40
Zuppa alla Marinara, 46
Zuppa di pesce alla Genovese, 46
Zuppa di pesce alla Siracusana, 48
Zuppa di pesce dei pescatori di Pozzuoli, 47
Zuppa Paradiso, 39
Zuppa Pavese, 38